D1544000

My Journey To
AMERICA

My Journey To
AMERICA

A Kurdish American Story

NEWZAD BRIFKI
Founder of Kurdish Community of America

NEXT CENTURY
PUBLISHING

My Journey To America
A Kurdish American Story

Published by Next Century Publishing
Las Vegas, Nevada
www.NextCenturyPublishing.com

ISBN: 978-1-68102-373-1

DEDICATION

To everyone who has inspired me throughout my journey and those who continue to do so.

ACKNOWLEDGMENTS

There are so many people I want to thank for helping me throughout my journey. First, my mother Fatima, who was always there for me, who supported and guided me through my life. She was both a mother and a father. She taught me the good from the bad and how to live a good life, loving everyone and everything. She always lectured me on how to get better, how to make the correct choices in life. She still continues to inspire me throughout my life. My mother always said, "You need to buy people." In other words, be good to them, do things for them even if it is for free. That is how you will get your name recognized. Also give bread to others. My mother also always told me, "When you have people over, treat them like kings and queens. Spoil them with food, drinks, and fine pastries. People will know you by what you give them and the good hospitality they get." My mother is my angel, my love, and everything; I don't know what I will do without her. May God protect her and keep her healthy until she meets my father and her parents again in heaven.

My brother Ismet, who is the oldest child. He was also like a father figure, protecting us siblings and giving us a new life in this country. It was he who helped us come to the United States. He wanted us to live a new life, to start a new beginning. Ismet has seen a lot in his life as well. He is very smart and always shared his ideas with us siblings. At a young age he became a Peshmerga, fighting for the Kurdish cause and helping the family out with the salary he received. He joined the Peshmerga when he was thirteen years old. The Kurdish Political Party, Kurdistan Democratic Party or KDP did not accept him as he was too young at that time. He did not give up and begged the Kurdistan Socialist Party to accept him. They allowed him to join their Peshmerga because their units were too small and they needed recruits. Later, one of my uncles, Sedeeq, who was a Peshmerga with the KDP, brought him with his unit to protect him as he was too young. Ismet got married at a young age. I believe he was around fifteen. The reason he got married at a young age was for his wife to help my mother in taking care of the family. He loves to hang out and loves people. He also likes to talk a lot about politics. Ismet speaks several languages even with little schooling. He speaks Arabic, Turkish, and is fluent in English and Kurdish.

I would like to thank my brother Khelat, who is like a best friend. At a young age he did not let me hang out with him but always looked after me. He was always there when I was going through a tough time, especially in heated moments. He was my protector and saved me a lot of times from getting beat up. He chased kids away when they tried to pick a fight with me. He has always been there for me and I can't thank him enough. Khelat loves to have a good time as well. He is not as social as Ismet when it comes to people, but he will do what we ask of him. He is also awesome with his hands. He has helped me a lot in the past, fixing things that I had no clue how to put together.

My sister, Dewlet, who lives in Kurdistan. She would always call and ask how I was doing. Whenever we went to visit Kurdistan she would treat me like a king. Even though her family didn't have much, she still provided good meals and good company. She always compliments me and says how everyone is proud of me for the work that I do and the intelligence that I have.

I would like to thank my sister Sarya for everything. Sarya has always been very kind and protective of me. When I was going through some tough times in South Dakota, she always helped out. She helped me pay for my braces and always gave me money. She was always supportive of me in my financial needs. Sarya is a cosmetologist and is super awesome in cutting hair. She is my personal stylist. She always lectures me on how to be a better person. There are no words to describe her. Sarya is super nice and when people, especially elderly folks, have a conversation with her, they fall in love with her personality right away.

Lastly in my family, I want to thank my sister Jihan. Jihan is like me in so many ways. She has gotten my back many times in the past. Jihan is very smart and motivated. She has always supported me. She has had my back in many fights even though she is a girl. Heck she even fought some battles for me. She fought guys who were twice my age and size. With the nonprofit that I started she helped out a lot in the beginning getting the word out and supporting me with many projects and events. She still continues to support me and inspire me. Even though Jihan and I have many differences we still get along great.

My family, as I mentioned has helped me a lot and because of them I am here today. My success is thanks to them supporting me in all my causes. Having strong family ties and support has been crucial to me being the best I can be. My family is only one part of my journey to thank.

Secondly, I want to thank my friends at an early age coming to the United States. Dan, Matt and Mike. Especially Dan. He was always a good friend and we never lost contact. We always kept in touch. I talk to Dan often and we hang out sometimes. He lives at the lake and is married now. Dan has always been like a brother. I will always be there for him as he was there for me. I want to thank Dan's parents, Jody and Tom. I want to also thank Matt's parents Julie and John who were the very best people who helped me at an early age. John and Julie truly gave me everything that a child could ask for. I will always be appreciative of them and will never forget what they did for me financially. I was new to the United States and had nothing. Dan and Matt's parents gave me what any kid could ask for and that was a happy childhood. Again I want to thank Dan, Matt and their parents for giving me happiness and making me forget about what had happened to me and what I went through at the refugee camp. I am thankful to them for taking me fishing, to church, to the lakes, to soccer practice, and the games we had. I will never forget the baseball games, sleepovers, and many other fun activities. I will hold all of them dear to my heart. May God help them with whatever they ask for and protect them. I pray that God will also grant them heaven when they leave this world.

Third, I want to thank my teachers for making me a great person, even though I bothered many of them by being a goofball in class. I am successful today because of them. My teachers would compliment me on my smile and say it will take you far in life. Teachers don't give up on their students. Special thanks to Mrs. Andrews and Mrs. Tweeten who were my ESL instructors, and were super nice and helpful. Karna at the YES program in Moorhead was also very nice and helpful. She helped me to finish and catch up on my credits that I needed to graduate high school. I want to thank my college instructors and professors who believed in me. They helped me when I asked and were supportive in ways I can't describe. Thank you to my teachers for the education you gave me.

Fourth, I want to thank Julian, the head of the DFL party in Moorhead. He inspired me to run for city council which I always had a passion for. I want to thank everyone who contributed to my campaign and for all the votes that they gave me. I will hopefully not let you down next time.

Fifth, I want to thank the United States of America and the American people for giving me a safe haven, a place where my family and I could have a new beginning. When no country opened their borders for us to live, the American people and the United States were there. The United

States is the greatest country in the world and I will debate with anyone who doesn't think so. I am very happy and thankful to be a part of this country. The country doesn't need to be great again it already is and only getting better. I want to thank the state of North Dakota for allowing refugee resettlement and placing us in Fargo. Also the state of Minnesota for being so supportive with social services. I am also thankful because I had the opportunity to go through the American education system.

Lastly, I want to thank the many service clubs in the Fargo-Moorhead area such as Rotary International and Kiwanis Club. These service clubs gave me a chance to tell my story which is what inspired me to write this book. If this book is successful I will give each of them a free copy that they can choose to keep or donate to any library of their choice.

Again, thank you to everyone who helped me throughout my journey. God bless you and the United States of America. May peace prevail on Earth.

CONTENTS

My Journey To
AMERICA

PROLOGUE

THROUGHOUT MY LIFE I had a calling. A calling to lead, to educate and to help others.

My life started leaving my home and taking refuge in a camp for four years. Later, my family and I would be relocated a thousand miles away from home. A place with new faces, language, and new society. I would come to the place where Lady Liberty says, "Give me your tired, your poor, your huddled masses yearning to breathe free, the wretched refuse of your teeming shore. Send these, the homeless, tempest-tossed to me: I lift my lamp beside the golden door!"

My family and I found America. In the United States I saw the good, the bad, and the ugly. I went through some tough times in dealing with poverty and being different in terms of having another cultural identity. Despite the prejudice from others who thought I was different, who made me feel uncomfortable and sad, I did not let it get to me because it was not physical harm, but rather psychological. Knowing that it was only psychological I had to be better than those uneducated people.

I have many American friends and they appreciate all the diversity here in this country. For example, if you look at some areas such as the military, hospitals, tech fields, sports, etc., they are all successful because of the diversity in them. They all play a part in making this country great because of their diversity and great minds. One will find diversity everywhere in this country, and it is because of this that the United States is so unique and great.

If a person is educated they accept others and know the history behind this country. The pilgrims came to America to seek religious freedom. Those whom are ignorant and self-centered have never really stepped out of their small little environment. They assume what they think is superior to others' way of thinking. These people think that they are only right. These ignorant people are really uneducated and don't know the beautiful world we live in. Yet the ignorant and uneducated people don't even know anything about the history of this great country nor all the different people in this world.

I have the United States and the American people to thank for my safe haven. Despite all the prejudice I went through growing up here I am still thankful for being safe. Having a roof over my head, food on the table and gaining the right education is what makes me appreciative and always looking at the positive side of this country. Not worrying about my house being bombed or someone physically harming me and my family is what matters. Even though growing up I did not have the best name-brand clothing to fit in with the other kids, I still had something to put on rather than just one pair of clothing like I did in the refugee camp I was living in prior to coming to the United States. Having food on the table was a blessing, even though at times it was not the best food. It still filled my stomach and I wasn't hungry like in the refugee camp.

I got an opportunity to get a good education in this country and that is one of my greatest achievements of which I'm appreciative. The education that I received prepared me to be a better person. I gained the right skills to use for my future goals and successes. If you talked to me on the phone I would sound like an ordinary American. If you see me I may look not white European but could go for many races. When people talk to me on the phone they don't ask where I am from, though when people see me face-to-face they question my identity.

I am trying to be a person that will bring good to humanity and the world. This is why I want to share my story. I will explain about the Middle East, religions that are there, and the various ethnic groups, specifically the Kurds. This book will hopefully be educational for you. With everything going on in the world in terms of terrorism, hate, wars, discrimination, injustice, hunger, disease, and natural disasters, this book will hopefully give you a chance to look at all these situations through my eyes.

I was always inspired to tell my story. I had shared some experiences with public schools, service clubs and other organizations, but I never had the chance to complete my story in a detailed way. I wanted to really share with others what it was like being a refugee and leaving everything behind. I had some opportunity to share my story but it was only for short period of time. Sometimes things get lost and forgotten when they are not written. This book will hopefully be available for anyone wanting to learn about another person's journey to America and their appreciation for it.

I was never really into books as a kid but did really like *To Kill a Mockingbird*. After college, I had an interest in reading about everything from religion to documentaries to wars and great leaders in history. By reading books I thought about my life's journey—all the things that I had gone through. What if I could document everything to educate others? I had done this before but through PowerPoint presentations, group talks, and having personal conversations with random people. However my audience was always small, and I hungered to educate more people. This book will hopefully do that. Even though I have been on TV and in the newspaper several times, I still think that this book would inspire many in reaching a bigger audience around the nation and hopefully around the world.

This book is full of my personal encounters, reflections, ideas, thoughts, and advice. A person can choose to take it whatever way they may but please do not get offended as this is only my personal view and I am not criticizing nor hating on anyone or anything. Lastly, I hope this will inspire those with a story to share with the world. This book will open new doors of opportunity for me. In this book, I will take you on a journey throughout my life, from leaving my beautiful homeland that I did not know existed, coming back to my homeland and feeling a cultural shock, taking me back in time fifty years. The most important reason behind this book is to share my story for you to learn about who I am. It will also hopefully educate you on what you can do to learn from others who have come from a different place and country to the United States.

This book is for me to really get everything out and reflect on my past. For me to document the many things that I witnessed and went through; the many things that I overcame, from bad to good. Learning to be better by not repeating the same mistakes. Lastly, to finally let go of everything inside me. To share my story with people around the world. To know and appreciate all the good things about the United States and the American people. In my personal opinion, Americans are the kindest people in the world because they truly care about others. They care because throughout the history of the world and conflicts, they have opened their doors to those who wanted to start a new life; those facing famine, natural disasters, war, and even those who just wanted to contribute to the American society. Allowing others to start a new life in the United States is what humanity is all about when other countries are so silent and deaf. Many of these immigrants will have a new beginning, where their children can have a future to believe in and have endless opportunities that they would not find anywhere else in the world.

With everything going on in the world we tend to hate on others because we have been taught this way. The media sometimes doesn't help by talking about small issues and turning them into big conflicts. The media tends to sometimes portray religious groups, races, and other ethnic groups as being different, inferior, and threatening. Mostly this tactic is used by politicians to scare the American people in voting for a specific person, as they will 'save them' from the so-called threat they are facing. Many times we humans do not use our own moral judgments but rather look to others, such as the media, to judge for us. Our leaders, who push us in the wrong direction, create chaos within. These so-called leaders make us think in the wrong way.

I promise you there are many like me in the United States who have come here to start a new life and truly appreciate everything that this country has given them. As I look back in my life I am very thankful for having the opportunity to be a part of this great nation. I always had an idea of writing a book and now is my opportunity to do so. It was just an idea floating in my head after I had done many presentations. When the North Dakota Humanities Council asked if I wanted to do a story on my refugee experience, it really pushed me to write this book. In their New American Edition I shared my story of my journey to America. After writing this piece and seeing it distributed all over the state of North Dakota, it made me want to appreciate myself for the talent that I had. To be honest, I really put my heart out writing that piece for them. Even though it was only around two-thousand words, it helped me to reflect on my past, present, and future. I have the skills to write, so I asked myself why not start writing a book?

This is how *My Journey to America* came to be. I hope that you will enjoy reading this book and that my journey will educate you. Again, everything in this book is from my personal experiences and opinions. I am no professional at giving advice nor telling it how it is. Yet everything that I express is simply to give you an idea of what I saw and did to become a better human being. I am very blessed to be a part of this nation and wish for my children to prosper as I have. Hopefully their future will be even riper than mine. Most of my life has been here in this country and the memories will always stay. Time flies and it seems like everything happened only yesterday. The number of years may seem too many but good memories never get old. From a baby to a child, a teenager to a young man. Now I am an adult in my thirties looking forward to fruitful days to come. May God bless us all for the good actions that we do. This book is about me, this book is a Kurdish American Story: My Journey to America.

CHAPTER 1

Who Am I?

I HAVE BEEN CALLED many names as a young man growing up in the United States. Names such as Heshak, George and Heja but my real name is Newzad Brifki. Newzad meaning 'new beginning', and Brifki is the town where I am from. My father named me Newzad when I was born but I was called Heja by family members later on. I was never really called Newzad, except when my family would receive international phone calls to the United States by my other family members in Kurdistan. They would ask to speak to me and called me using the name Newzad.

After learning that my name was always Newzad and that my father had named me personally, it was something that I wanted to change when given the opportunity. That is the name he gave me but he never had the chance to see me grow up with that name. For this reason I wanted my name to be changed back to Newzad from Heja to remember my father who I didn't get a chance to know. My father was always talked about as having been a good, wise man. I wanted to remember his legacy and greatness, which is why I decided to change my name and later follow in his footsteps. In the book *48 Laws of Power*, Robert Greene mentions, "Be yourself because to be like your father and to intimate his greatness you have to do twice the work to even get a little of the recognition." This may be true and I may never become like my father, though that is not my purpose. I don't want to be like him nor do exactly what he did. I want to just follow some of his good traits by which to remember him and know whose son I am.

My mother became a naturalized citizen after I turned eighteen. Anyone who is over eighteen must take the naturalization test or U.S. history test which consists of about one-hundred questions. Therefore, I had to take the civics test for my naturalization which was a piece of cake, though I think most Americans today wouldn't know the answer to half of the questions. It is a good test though and one which I think is very important to have. Coming from another country and becoming the citizen of this country allows individuals to appreciate this country better by knowing its history and founding fathers. If my mother would have been a citizen before my eighteenth birthday I would have become an automatic citizen and not have had to take the civics test. Even though I didn't mind taking the test, things would have been easier if I would have become an automatic citizen. My naturalization was delayed for several years because of some trouble I had with law enforcement for a citation I received and didn't report on my application. I had to wait five years from the time I applied for naturalization.

After getting a chance to be a naturalized citizen, I changed my name from Heja to Newzad in 2008. This was a great feeling and I was really honored to be called Newzad after that. I felt different and good that finally I was called what my father had named me. I was going to honor my father by giving him the best son he never got to see become a man. I wanted people to say, 'Newzad, the son of Reshid; wow, he truly has taken after him or at least some of his greatness. He is kind—a leader and someone we can look up to.' My mom would always say stories about my father. He was a great man. He loved his country, his people, and was always a problem solver. According to my mother, my father was like a judge because back some years ago the place I was born and where I am from was a total chaos of war and instability. I am from a place called Kurdistan, a region in the Middle East.

Technically Kurdistan does not exist as an independent country—it was split into four countries (northern Iraq, southern Turkey, eastern Syria, and western Iran) after the collapse of the Ottoman Empire during World War I by the Sykes-Picot Agreement. The Sykes-Picot agreement betrayed the Kurds because they were promised their own homeland after the collapse of the Ottoman Empire, but that never came to be. In the Middle East, there are different ethnic groups and religions that reside there. When we see the news all we think of sometimes is Israel and Palestine. We think of Saudi Arabia and Iran. Most people think the Middle East is all Islam. That is not the case. You have Kurds, Turks, Persians, Arabs, and Jews all living in the Middle East. The religions consist of Animism, Zoroastrianism, Yezidism, Judaism, Christianity, Islam and many other minority religions.

Ever since the secret treaty between France, England, and Turkey, Kurdish people have been oppressed under these brutal governments and dictators of Iraq, Syria, Iran and Turkey. The conflict has lasted for almost a century. The Kurds are of the Aryan race. They were born from the time of Mesopotamia, an Indo-European people with their own religion, customs, and culture. The Kurds are a brave race that have always been fierce warriors. The Kurds are known for fighting throughout history against tyrannies. The Kurds are the ones who destroyed the Assyrian empire in 612 BC, who used to rule half of the Middle East and Southwestern Asia. The Assyrians were brutal people and their empire had no mercy over anyone. Tired of tyranny, the Kurds assembled themselves and took over the Assyrian empire, collapsing it and creating the Mesopotamian Empire. With different tribes, empires, and religious attacking the Kurds. They got used to fighting.

The Kurds became a victim of each attack, having to stand up against many forces and rulers to save their heritage, culture, and people. They sometimes won battles but were also oppressed and betrayed, causing oppression. There is a saying that the Kurds have no friends but the mountains and having learned this lesson. The Kurdish people had to really protect themselves throughout these various eras. Rulers such as Alexander the Great, the Persian Empire, the religious crusades of Christianity and Islam, and finally the Ottoman Empire all tried to squash and force the Kurdish people to bow to their feet. At times when the Kurds were weak, they surrendered because there was no other choice if they wanted to survive. The Kurds did try to assimilate into these empires and rulers but they also stayed true to their identity. Real Kurds with honor have never bowed to any man except God. Any chance they got, they destroyed their enemy.

If you look at the map of the Middle East today, I would be labeled as being from Iraq or from the Kurdistan Region of Iraq. They would call me an Iraqi. My mother tongue is not Arabic, my culture is different than Arabs, and the way the Kurds view the world and humanity is different than the Arab race. So why should I consider myself as an Iraqi? I am a Kurd from Kurdistan. My people are totally different than Persians, Arabs, and Turks; it is like comparing an apple to an orange. We are a proud people and do respect the Persians, Arabs, and Turks, but we will never bow down to them and they will never rule us. Why should we be the weaker link, the inferior race? We are a proud people that have held on to our culture and ideas for thousands of years. We used to have an empire but because of repeated betrayal it collapsed along with other great moments of Kurdish nationalism. We have our own language and customs. We wish to live in peace with these neighbors but also want our own independent country. As Turkey, Iran, Iraq and Syria love their country, we love ours too and it's called Kurdistan. It is much prettier, wealthier, and the society thinks like the west. At no time in history except for the Mede Empire have the Kurds been as noticed as today. With the help of technology and social media the Kurds have gotten their recognition in the world. Some years ago, our voices were shut by these regimes and we were labeled as non-existing people.

I was born in Duhok, Kurdistan, on October 12, 1984 in a small village forty minutes away from the city. I was not born in a hospital, and the survival rate of children was small—as well as for the mother. We had no doctors, no medicine; such supplies were rare. Those who helped to give labor to the pregnant women were mostly midwives or those individuals who studied a little bit of medicine.

I am the youngest of six siblings. I had two other brothers but they died. One was named Mohammed; he died at the age of five and the other was Newzad who died at the age of two. Sometimes I wonder how they died. My mother does not know either. She said, "They both got sick and later died." I assume because there were no vaccinations, no child checkups, or medicine. That there was a great potential for the risk of death amongst the children when they got sick. My family was not the only one who lost children. The lack of medicine and care that was needed for children and individuals was not available. The medicine available was mostly made by medicine men.

My other sibling's names are Ismet, Dewlet, Sarya, Khelat, and Jihan. Ismet is the oldest living child. He is like a father figure. He has always been there for us and watched over us. It was him who encouraged my mother to take the journey to America and start a new life. He helped with all the paperwork and arranged everything for us to come to the United States. Ismet is a very smart man. He knows a lot of people and is respected by many. Sometimes he can be very hardheaded and to debate with him is difficult because when you're with him it is always his way; he is the one who is right all the time. Dewlet lives in Kurdistan. She got married before coming to the United States and therefore she was not able to come with us. She is a sweet woman and likes to write poems in Kurdish. Sarya is a generous person. She likes to help out people in any way she can. She loves her reputation for being a good woman and takes after my mother when it comes to holding on to the family and savings for the future. Khelat is my cool brother. He is like a friend. He loves to have fun and likes to joke. He is a hard worker and is good with his hands. He can get easily upset because he does not tolerate lies and people with big egos. Jihan is my other sister. She loves to shop and hang out with friends. She has company over all the time and when people are not at her house she is at theirs. She is very patriotic when it comes to the Kurdish cause and has helped me a lot with my non-profit that I founded called the Kurdish Community of America.

All of my siblings are married and have children. They all live in the same city as me in Moorhead, except for Dewlet; she lives in Duhok, Kurdistan. We are trying to help Dewlet and her family to come here as well. Her husband Faisal's brother, Faiq, worked with the United States Army during Operation Iraqi Freedom. He got a visa to come to the United States. Therefore Faiq is able to bring other family members and we are trying to help them out this way.

For myself, I am married with three kids. My wife's name is Sheelan. We have two girls, Peyvin and Lorin, and recently had a son, Perwer. I helped Sheelan's family to come to the United States as well. They came here under the same program as Faiq did, because Sheelan's father, Anwar, worked for the United States government thanks to my brother giving him a security job. They are living here now after a long process of applying and security background checks. I married Sheelan because of my first experiment visiting Kurdistan. Since we fled in 1988 during the Kurdish genocide I had not returned back. Sheelan is from the same town as me. Seeing her family I felt very sorry for them. Sheelan had five other sisters and three brothers, which was a big family for only her father to support. Her father worked but it was not enough to help all of them out. I got to know Sheelan after my trip and thought the best thing for me to do was to ask if she wanted to get married. This way I could help her start a new life in the United States and sometimes send money to her family, which was very poor. I talked to my brother, who talked to her parents as this is our tradition and way of getting the parents' permission before marriage would be announced.

Fargo, ND and Moorhead, MN are sister cities that border the Red River which floats south out of Canada. It is a good place to live and raise a family. Even though it is extremely cold here in the winter time it is a good, quiet place. It is easy to get anywhere in about fifteen minutes. The summers here are awesome weather; not too hot, with a little wind. With Minnesota being the land of ten-thousand lakes, there is plenty of fun in the summer. I ask myself sometimes if I am going to be here my whole life. That is a good question because I have many goals in mind. I would like to pursue bigger things in life and continue my public service work in politics. I am a hard-headed person when it comes to reaching my goals. I like to work hard and be a leader. I am always on top of the game. I don't like to lose, and if I do lose, I show that I fought a tough battle. I am always looking for new endeavors.

I like to put it into these words: I am Columbus of America trying to land on the right opportunity. I gained a lot of knowledge throughout my life. I got a chance to get a good education and currently hold a Master's degree in Business Administration. I have learned much from my mistakes and from what I went through as a child living in a refugee camp. I can at times get upset very easily. I try to control my anger and have gotten better through different techniques such as breathing exercises or going for a walk. I don't like liars or thieves. I believe that anyone has the potential to be anything if given the chance. Many people are jealous or envy each other which is why many times they don't give another person an opportunity. People should not be judged by how they look or where they are from but rather what their background is. They should be judged by their experiences and what their character is like.

So who am I? I am a good person who loves life. I love everything about this world. The people, nature, countries, cultures, the arts, music, and more than I can write down. I am a person who likes to learn. I am always looking for ways to learn a new language, a new culture, meet a new person. I love to learn a new subject. The most desirable is learning about history. History teaches about different people, faiths, customs, and how the world shaped itself today.

Looking at politics I can't say that I am from a specific party. I ran for Moorhead City Council in 2013 as a Conservative Democrat thanks to Julian Dahlquist for encouraging me. However I was defeated because of the lack of experience that I had in politics. Even though I got a quite a few votes I could have done better and won if I would have tried harder. Later I would change my political view from Democrat to Republican. I truly value the Republican Party and especially because it was founded by Abraham Lincoln, one of the most respected presidents of the United States.

Republicans are good at what they do and they don't lie. If something is not right they will say it clear and loud. As for Democrats, they only care about votes and don't want to hurt anyone's feelings even though they have their own agenda. I believe in the Republican Party but what I thought was very strange was that the party chose Donald Trump to be their presidential nominee. Trump has some issues when it comes to saying everything at all times. I am not saying that he isn't qualified to be president. It's just sometimes a person has to watch their mouth and not let everything out despite what is in their hearts.

I truly understand where Trump is coming from. There are too many people who want to hurt the United States. This does not mean though that we should create fear within our people and make the society uncivilized and racist. Trump argues that it is the Muslims and the religion of Islam who is at fault. It is not the religion of Islam, however; it is the Muslims who preach terroristic ideas that hurt mankind and destabilize societies. The few who make the Islam religion look bad do not represent the religion and are only doing these bad things for their own personal gains. The problem is when you have uneducated people, their brains are not able to think critically nor rationally and they will listen to someone who says go blow yourself up so you can go to heaven and leave this filthy world. Immigrants are a part of the United States' history. As it is a country of immigrants, we must be respectful at all times and allow anyone to come here when it comes to legal immigration and the right background checks.

This country is great because of the great minds that move it forward and contribute to it. Trump, I am sorry but you have to do better than this if you want to lead the best country in the world. I do like Trump though, as he has mentioned that the Kurds are in the frontlines against ISIS. So Mr. Trump, thank you for that. However I don't agree with Trump when he said that "it was okay for Saddam to use a little chemical gas." That was a very disrespectful comment, especially to the Kurdish people. Saddam Hussein used his chemical gas that killed thousands of innocent Kurds, with the city of Halabja as the center of the gas attacks. Other cities and villages were bombed with chemicals in the Kurdistan Region. Halabja was hit the hardest; there were over five thousand fatalities within minutes, not to mention the thousands who were severely injured by the gas and still have birth defects because of it to this day.

Lastly, I want Trump to know that he should know how this country was started. It was the Pilgrims who came here seeking religious freedom. Insulting Islam is not only inappropriate but unconstitutional, as the First Amendment protects all religions practiced in this country. 2016 will be a historical election year, as Trump will face the first woman nominee: Hillary Clinton. Hillary Clinton may be a good president but there are some things in my own opinion that she needs to do. It would not be wise for her to repeat the same mistakes as the Obama Administration did with foreign policy. The Democrats stink at foreign policy even though I do give them credit for being good to the country within.

The fact of the matter is we need a strong president who will be tough in foreign policy. I say this because the United States is the police of the world. Whether it likes it or not, this country has given itself this name. Therefore, it has to do its job if it wants to continue being a superpower in the world. The United States has to protect countries and people oppressed by dictators and unjust governments. If the United States does not do this we will be looked at as weak and someone else might do the job for us. So whether Trump or Hillary becomes president, they need to change their policies. If Trump is elected, he needs to come out as a little softer with the United States, to prevent the people in it from turning against one another and to respect each other as Americans. He has to change his tone and hate. Hillary, if elected, has the experience already to lead the United States but she needs to change her foreign policy. She cannot be soft on Turkey, Saudi Arabia, and Iran. She cannot be soft with North Korea, Cuba, and Venezuela. She cannot allow Russia and China to lead the world as they are only partners or associates and not the superpower of the world. Hillary needs to become a tough woman and sometimes even act like a man.

My hopes and dreams for the future is to be able to take part in such decision making. I will run for office continuing my public service work for the people. What I will run for will be determined, and how long it will take is a question. Though I must continue to have faith in God as he will lead me to the position I am destined for.

CHAPTER 2

Leaving Home

THE CREATION OF the so called Middle Eastern countries that we see and hear about today was the cause and effect during the collapse of the Ottoman Empire after WWI. The countries of Iraq, Syria, Turkey, and Iran were divided amongst themselves by the British and French. Soon these countries revolted and kicked the British and French out. Ever since, there has been conflict between these regimes and governments towards their own people and mainly towards the Kurdish population. These four countries, fearing that the Kurds would unite one day and ask for their own state, oppressed them severely from accomplishing anything in the future. At times, when given the opportunity, Kurds did revolt and tried to unite in having their own state. These four countries already had plans in place for Kurds if they tried to revolt and ask for their own state. Each time Kurdistan tried to become a separate country the chances of success were very slim. The Kurds failed each time because of no outside support. They were surrounded by the enemy and with no way out there only option was to surrender for another day.

In these four countries, the Kurds fought for an independent state of their own but primarily for more rights, such as to speak in their native tongue, to practice their religions, and to celebrate their cultural identity. These countries oppressed the Kurds so much that in Turkey the Kurdish language was banned; in Syria their citizenship was stripped, making them look like Gypsies, and they could not hold any successful positions. In Iran hangings by the government were becoming a normal routine; even today, many youths are hanged to scare the Kurdish population. In Iraq, the Kurds were forced into military and sentenced to be tortured when they did not accept the Arabization taking place in their villages, towns, cities, schools, and everyday life.

Despite all the attempts with these countries' governments and regimes, they failed to change the Kurds' hope of an independent state. The Kurds did not give up and haven't given up, even though they lost much of everything—their homes, their families, and most of all their honor to defend their homes. The successful Kurds were in Northern Iraq, the area where I am from. They were led by Mustafa Barzani, the head of the Kurdistan Democratic Party (KDP) founded in 1946, a branch of Qazi Mohammed's party, Kurdistan Democratic Party of Iran (KDPI). Qazi Mohammed declared the Republic of Mahabad in Kurdistan, Iran. It became a country for almost a year and as things were turning out to be good for the Kurdistan nation Qazi Mohammed was later hanged that year by the Iranian regime on March 31st, 1947 after the Russian allies betrayed him. The Russian government betrayed Kurdistan and Qazi Mohammed's Kurdish government by not supporting him, though they were allies at that time both against the Iranian regime.

Mustafa Barzani escaped Kurdistan, Iran after the murder of Qazi Mohammed. Mustafa Barzani being from Kurdistan Region of Iraq in the area of Barzan went back after Qazi Mohammed's death. He started unifying Kurds of Iraq from all parts in Kerkuk, Hewler, Suleymani, and Duhok, to join his revolution against the Iraqi government for more rights and autonomy. The war lasted many years and despite little fire power and recruits, the leader Mustafa Barzani and his Peshmerga were efficient fighters with the mountains as their advantage and safe haven.

Just like the Patriots of the United States during the Revolutionary War against the British, the Peshmerga used the same tactic; a hit-and-run strategy. This strategy was also successful during the civil war of China between the Nationalists and Communists from 1927 to 1950, where the Nationalist Party had the firing power but the Communists had a better strategy of war, in which their hit-and-run tactics worked humiliating the Nationalist Party.

After many years, the Iraqi government promised the Kurds more autonomy and rights in their region if they stopped the hit-and-run fighting. The Kurdish Peshmerga agreed and there was a ceasefire between the two for several months, with the Iraqi government talking about more rights for its citizens but not taking any action to put them into play. The Kurds had enough talk and the ceasefire did not last long. Later, another monster would emerge as the new leader of the Baath Party in Iraq; his name would be Saddam Hussein, a Sunni Arab.

Saddam Hussein assassinated the Iraqi president and became the dictator of Iraq in 1979 claiming himself as the new president of Iraq. His image was the same as Hitler's—his campaign was no different, either. Wanting to control the whole Middle East just like Hitler wanted to control all of Europe. The Kurds once again had to take up arms and fight the Iraqi government but this time the brutal dictator had no mercy. Saddam put an agenda on his table to crush the Kurds of Iraq that did not follow him. Fighting between the Kurds and Saddam's government turned into a genocide in the year of 1988. Saddam Hussein ordered his half-brother Chemical Ali, or Majeed Ali, to use weapons of mass destruction. He named his new campaign 'Al-Anfal', a verse in the scriptures of the holy book Quran used by Islam; translated, it means 'Spoils of War'.

Saddam was fighting Iran over almost a decade and he had enough. He blamed the Kurds for not winning the war in which both countries had lost hundreds of thousands of men. He used chemical gas on the Iranian army and the Kurdish population. The biggest area that was hit was Halabja a Kurdish city, which had nothing to do with the Iraq and Iran war. All civilians living in the city were gassed; over five-thousand died instantly. Several thousand others were injured by blindness, third degree burns, and obstruction of the airway.

The Kurds were always fierce warriors but there was no way in fighting chemical. After Saddam saw that his chemical attack frightened people, he ordered more to be dropped in other Kurdish cities and villages where the Peshmerga were located. The chemical was in the air so we had no choice but to run as fast as we could. When the Kurdish Peshmerga would take in prisoners of Arab fighters they would feed them food, give them safety, and send them back to their families. Not the Baath Regime of Saddam. He declared an all-out war on the Peshmerga and the Kurds in which more than two-hundred-thousand were brutally executed by firing squads, hangings, beatings, gas attacks, torture, being buried alive, and other things that are inhuman to describe. My father was one of the victims of the Baath Regime's campaigns; he was killed in 1985 in an ambush by some of their members, on top of the hundreds of thousands of deaths. Many were injured or paralyzed and have severe mental health issues today because of the war.

~

After our home was destroyed by Iraqi bombs, we had no choice but to leave. I remember being a child on the shoulders of my brother carrying me as I was too young and could not walk through the mountain terrain. I remember his AK-47 rifle jamming me in the stomach. I wanted to tell him I was hurting but realized if I did that I had to walk. So despite the pain, which I can remember today, I stayed quiet then. We tried to flee into Kurdistan, Turkey, but the Turkish government refused to allow us in. We spent several days stranded with no food and water, and several children and the elderly refugees died as a result. I remember resting by a stream and being very hungry along with my family surrounding me. My family had yogurt but no bread as we did not have enough time to pack our things when we fled the bombings. The yogurt and other vegetation around us is all we ate for a couple of days. The genocide of the Kurds had reached the outside. Many of the ex-patriot Kurds who lived in western countries pressured their governments with protests and meetings with government officials to rescue those stranded on the mountains.

Finally our prayers were answered when we saw American and coalition planes flying above us dropping food and supplies for the refugees stranded on the Turkish border. Chaos started as pallets of food and supplies smashed the mountainside from the air and the people rushed to it to get as much as they could for their families. Sometimes the pallets would crush those whom were not patient for it to land. This was an ugly situation and sounds kind of nuts, but being hungry and not knowing you will survive, humans can get out of control. Everyone was worried about their lives and their families. No one knew how long they would be stranded on the mountains. This is why when food and supplies were dropped, many rushed to gather whatever rations they could to help themselves survive for days to come. The American and Coalition planes had no choice but to drop the food from the air. There was no place to land on the steep mountainside. After being stranded on the Turkish border for many days, the western countries pressured Turkey into allowing us to enter as refugees. The Turkish government was not happy but had no choice but to agree to whatever deal was made, being a NATO country.

They finally allowed the refugees to enter under one condition: we had to be placed in concentration camps surrounded by their soldiers. No one was allowed in or out without the Turkish soldiers' permission. The Turkish soldiers finally allowed the refugees to enter but not with politeness. Many individuals were sworn at, spit on, and hit by rifles and their boots. Why would someone want to leave their home in such a situation?

We had everything in Kurdistan. Even though my family was living in a village we still survived and had everything we wanted. The village where I was born is a beautiful one, full of orchard trees and clean mountain stream water that you can drink with the palm of your hands. Nice shade by the trees that when the wind hits the leaves melts your heart away. You don't need an AC to cool off, in the area I am from. All you need is some shade from the beautiful trees that will protect a person from the sun on hot summer days.

My mother would tell me that the Peshmerga would be at my house by the hundreds. Other friends and family from other villages visited us as well. No one in the village had any supplies really and my dad was the only one who had a market that provided all those things that the villagers and visitors needed. It was a war between the Kurds and Arabs, between Iraq and Kurdistan. They controlled everything and called all the shots. We still had everything, despite it all. I will not speak on behalf of all Kurds, but I can say that the majority are good people. They did not want to leave their homes. Now they are living all over the world, far from Kurdistan. Yet most of them still dream of a Kurdish state. Even though they left many of them have built a new home in the United States, Canada, the United Kingdom, Sweden, Germany, Australia, and many other developed countries. These countries have given them a safe haven, an education, a chance for a new beginning. They have provided them with everything they need. All they have to do is just live and be happy.

This is why the Kurds and I myself are so appreciative of these and many other countries, which took the Kurdish people as refugees when no one else did. The Kurds are ninety-nine percent Muslim and not even one of the Muslim countries gave them a safe haven or refugee resettlement. We know this and will never forget this kindness from these developed countries. This is why in the Kurdistan Region of Iraq we see over 1.5 million refugees from all ethnic groups and religions due to the current situation in Syria, Turkey, Iran and Iraq.

The autonomous Kurdistan Region is only about six million in population and this huge number of refugees has devastated everything. Everything from their economy to jobs to resources becoming scarce.

With Baghdad controlling most of the funds it is hard on the Kurdish Regional Government and its people to help these refugees let alone themselves. However, the Kurds, as I mentioned, are good people. Despite the many hardships they still continue to help these refugees as they were in this situation. I pray that Kurdistan becomes independent. Iraq is a failed state and will never become one unified country. After ISIS falls there will be talk once again of a unified Iraq. This is a wrong approach because even if the Kurds don't secede from Iraq there will still be conflict between Sunni Arabs backed by Saudia Arabia and Shia Arabs that are backed by Iran. They hate each other and will never be one. It will only bring Kurds into their pathetic conflict.

The only solution is for Iraq to be three separate states: Shiites in the South, Sunnis in the Middle, and Kurds will have their own state of Kurdistan. This is the only solution for Iraq. Imagine having three flower vases. You drop two, Sunnis and Shiites, and they break. You are left with one: the Kurds. What is the best option? Is it best to try to put the other vases that are already broken back together or should you go with the vase that is intact? The correct agenda for the United States and other countries is to support the Kurds and Kurdistan. If you want boots on the ground, you have them. If you want an ethnic group in the region next to Israel that will be loyal, you will have the Kurds and Kurdistan. The Kurds are already an established nation. They have their own military, parliament, and flag. The only thing left for them is to have their own currency and recognition from the outside as an independent country. Look at those fighting ISIS on the front lines. It is the brave Kurdish forces from the Kurdistan Region of Syria and Iraq, Rojava, and Bashur. Maybe Rojava and Bashur can unite and hopefully claim a Kurdish independent state. They will still be missing two pieces from the Kurdistan Region of Iran: Rojhelat, and the biggest part in Turkey, Bakur—though having a couple of pieces of the pie is better than nothing.

When the time comes, the Kurdistan Regions of Turkey and Iran can unite with Bashur and Rojava again, being the once dominating force of the Mede Empire. This was why I left home and my beautiful Kurdistan. I pray that one day Kurdsitan will fly their flag next to all the other nations in the world.

CHAPTER 3

Life in the Refugee Camp

THE LUXURY OF all the things we have today for everyday use is truly remarkable. Hot running water to wash clothes and bathe. Cold water to drink and swim, grocery stores and markets that have shelves full of food. Good doctors and medicine to treat illnesses. Schools that are clean and where one can actually focus on their studies. Our lights are on all the time when we need it in our developed countries.

These are some of the things that we enjoy every day. We should not be just happy, but grateful. Many people around the world don't have these things. Heck, it is even a luxury for some people to have these things in a third world country. That was my life and situation; I didn't have these things in the refugee camp. We didn't have these luxuries, and when we did have them, it was something to be grateful about because it was only for a short period of time.

Life in the refugee camp was very hard. Imagine being left out in the middle of nowhere. Where grass did not grow, where there was no water line, no electricity and the basic necessities of everyday were a treasure. Those of us living in the refugee camp in Mardin, Turkey were given small rations of food. Most families were given one loaf of bread per day, so little that it barely fed one person yet alone a whole family of six with two adults and four children. Imagine having one loaf of bread for the whole day and not even being able to make a sandwich.

I still can't imagine today what life was like in the refugee camp. Now I eat breakfast, lunch, and dinner and sometimes have snacks in between. I look back and wonder how we even survived four years of life at the refugee camp in Turkey. I remember sneaking out of the camp with other kids when the Turkish soldiers (Jendermah) would take breaks. We would go to nearby villages, walking for hours to ask for bread. Many times we got chased by the villagers' dogs and came back empty-handed. No wonder I am so afraid of dogs today—even though most of the dogs here in America are very nice and well-mannered. Still the fear from my past makes me think that any dog could attack me. When I see dogs, especially mean-looking ones, I get flashbacks of those vicious ones who use to chase us when we snuck out of the camp. Many of those dogs were sheepdogs of the nearby townspeople, so coming close to them, even within seventy-five feet, would be very dangerous. This, however, did not stop us.

We kids were in a bad situation and even though we were afraid of the dogs attacking us, that didn't stop us from going into the nearby villages from time to time to ask for food. At times we were lucky and received bread from the local villagers near our camp. We knocked on many doors and most of the time they drove us away by shutting the door on us. The villagers who did give us bread were good people. Even though the bread was old, hard, and sometimes moldy, we did not care; it was delicious for us because we were hungry. It was like eating a piece of steak or apple pie because food was a treasure. That bread was all we had and we enjoyed every piece of it. I thank those families for opening their doors and giving us bread.

Other times, we hunted birds and grilled their meat. It sounds kind of gross, especially because we had no spices such as salt to make it have more favorable. It was all the meat that we had and at that time we did not complain. In the refugee camp we did not get meat. I believe chicken was the only meat distributed once every six months for the families. It was only one chicken feeding a huge family. So the birds we caught and ate were enough to satisfy us. When you saw a kid with a sling shot, it was for the birds. We shot at the birds, grilled them, and that was about it. It was not much but it helped out then with a little bit of protein that we needed to be strong and maintain our energy.

Fortunately, I was never caught by the Turkish soldiers. If kids were caught they got beat up pretty bad to instill fear into us so we wouldn't leave the camp grounds. There are many stories that I hear from other family members who were caught by the Jendermah. The kids that got caught got slapped, kicked, and whipped by the Jendermah's rifles. Even though some kids got caught and beat up by the Turkish soldiers, this didn't prevent them from continuing to sneak out of the refugee camp.

Until one day there was a horrific incident.

A couple of young guys went out of the camp to a nearby village. They ended up getting into an argument with an older man from the village. The older man had a heart attack afterwards and died. Not knowing what to do, the young guys came running back into the camp. The Jendermah knew about the incident and chased the young guys into the camp. The young guys were too fast for the soldiers and so that is when the gunshots happened. The Jendermah shot at the young kids with rifle bullets bursting into the campground. I was sitting next to an old, heavier man at my brother Ismet's café that he started at the camp. I saw that old man just drop to the ground with blood all over him. People started yelling, screaming and crying. There was chaos all over the camp. Luckily, my brother-in-law Faisal grabbed me and brought me inside.

Ismet, coming out of his tent to see what was happening, got shot in the lower rib and arm. One person got killed and several others got injured with bullet wounds by the Jendermah. This was a scary situation.

After this incident the camp was on lockdown most of the time. Going out of the camp after this incident was only acceptable with permission from the Jendermah. I remember many nights sleeping hungry and even eating grass at the nearby villages. Food was only one of the many things that we didn't have at the refugee camp. Hygiene supplies were scarce. We took showers once a week, if that. Because of the lack of shampoo, soap, and washing clothes, my feet became infected being barefooted all the time. We didn't have tennis shoes or different pairs of socks to put on. If we were lucky we had one shoe and that was an ugly fake leather shoe. The shoe wouldn't last a week and most people sewed their shoe back together. At times when it was really hot out, the shoe was leather but wasn't the real thing and it would melt. This caused people to get burned by the shoe with the fake leather melting on their feet. Being barefooted caused my feet to be infected as well. I got cut several times and with no antibiotics and bandages, it got infected.

I was sick all the time and because there was no medicine to get healed, it felt like forever. There was no clothing or running water. We didn't change our clothes every day because we didn't have many to put on. We took a bath probably once a week if we were lucky because of the lack of water. This was a devastating situation. Imagine how important water is and not having it for everyday use. Kids went without changing their clothes because they had none. Mothers had to deal with the little children when they made a mess of themselves and could not change them because they had no clothes or water. The water well was about a half-mile away and when the well water was open there was fighting between everyone trying to be the first to get it. Canned vegetable containers that were about four gallons were the only way to store water. The vast amount of people in the camp made it harder to get enough water for families to store. It was very hard to get enough water to drink and use it for other daily needs.

The lack of water and clothing was only one part of trying to survive. I remember that we would roll up our socks—we had only had one pair each—and use it as a soccer ball. This was the only ball that we had. There were no toys or playground. We played games such as hide and seek, five rocks (berkane), and if one was lucky they had a few marbles. As you may see already, I did not have a fun childhood in the refugee camp.

Our tents were in horrible condition, and we barely had anything to sleep on or to cover ourselves with at night. Many of the children and elderly could not bear the cold and died. When there was a storm, our tents flew everywhere and with no supplies to fix them; they were in horrible condition and torn apart.

There is a film that was recorded during my stay in the Mardin refugee camp. If you visit the following link on YouTube with your own eyes you will see the devastation: **https://www.youtube.com/watch?v=RsU3SkhRmVE**.

You will see the situation and how bad it was for us. This video captures only some moments in the refugee camp and not all the other horrific scenes. With limited supplies made things even harder for people and families. As I mentioned it was very difficult because many families had lots of children, and the limited supplies did not feed, warm, or cleanse everyone. Winter and rainy seasons were the worst in the refugee camp. We children had no toys and the mud was our only playground. Supplies came late all the time and not enough came. When food came, many people got sick and even died of food poisoning. We did not know if the food was poisoned on purpose or because it was expired.

Rumors in the camp spread that the Turkish government was sick of us and wanted to kill us off. They were especially getting frustrated with the Iraqi Kurds because of their own Kurdish population being influenced by speaking Kurdish. The Kurds of Iraq showed them many things that they had forgotten about their cultural identity. The Kurds of Turkey were in a horrible situation as well; they were horribly oppressed and their native language had been banned. Speaking Kurdish was a crime in Turkey and one could go to jail if it was heard. For the Kurds in Turkey hearing the Kurdish language was a relief and happiness. Even though many had lost the language and could not speak it anymore they were still happy saying some words and hearing their native tongue.

At the camp there was no doctors around and when they came, people lined up for over a mile to see one. The doctors came for certain things and were there once a month, if that. We had nurse practitioners from Kurdistan Region of Iraq but because they lacked the medicine and supplies to help the sick, there was not much that could be done to treat patients. Due to this, many died, especially the elderly and infants.

My family and I spent a whole four years in the camp. Even in the best circumstances, camping is only fun for a few days, not four years. During the last year of our stay at the refugee camp, humanitarian organizations from the United States and other western countries came. A couple of Lutheran families from Fargo, North Dakota sponsored my family to start a new life in the United States. We came to the United States on September 21, 1992, when I was seven years old, and that is how my life started in America.

I still remember today Serdar, my cousin who was killed during the Kurdish civil war that started in the Kurdistan Region of Iraq in the mid 1990s. The civil war was between the Kurdistan Workers' Party (PKK), the Kurdistan Democratic Party (PDK), and the Patriotic Union of Kurdistan (PUK). The civil war was over which party would take control of the new autonomous Kurdistan Region of Iraq. The PDK had the most experience as a political party, both diplomatically and during wartimes. The leader, Masoud Barzani, the son of Mustafa Barzani, was now in charge of the party. Masoud is the current president of the autonomous Kurdistan Region of Iraq. The leader of the PKK was Abdula Ocalan from Kurdistan Region of Turkey; his party was supposed to be involved in the affairs of the Kurds in Turkey and not Iraq. Then there was Jalal Talabani the head of the PUK.

The civil war lasted for a couple of years and as my own personal statement the other two parties are to blame. The PKK was not happy that the PDK was working with Turkey on trade. Well, what were they supposed to do, starve their people? The PUK was not happy that the PDK had the most seats in the Kurdish Parliament and that the newly elected president was the son of Mustafa Barzani. Well the people chose Masoud to be their president. They had an election and he won. So in a nutshell the civil war should have not happened but it did and thousands of innocent Kurdish lives were lost by their own brothers. When we were leaving the camp, Serdar came rushing to me and asked where my brother Khelat was? I told him I did not know. He looked at me as I was getting into the bus, smiled, and said, "Tell your brother I will miss him." He gave me some Turkish Lira, the money that is used in Turkey. That was the last time I saw Serdar again and the last time I saw the refugee camp.

Our last photo at the camp, prior to coming to America.

CHAPTER 4

Coming to America

W<small>HEN</small> I <small>ARRIVED</small> in the United States for the first time, it was snowing big time in Fargo, North Dakota. Everything was white, covered with snow. Driving from the airport all I did was stare; everything looked different and strange. I was trying to figure everything out. I had seen snow before and I was used to it. Though in my mind I thought even the snow here was different, which made me curious. What was it? Why was everything different?

One thing that caught my eye coming from the airport was that I had never seen so many cars before. It was really something amazing. It was a luxury to be in a vehicle before coming to America. I had been in a car once throughout my life. That was at the refugee camp. It started out with my sister Dewlet and her husband Faisal going to some kind of appointment that they had in Diyarbakir, which was a couple of hours away from the Mardin refugee camp. At a rest stop, we got out and had some snacks. Faisal gave me a banana to eat. It was the first banana that I ever had and it was delicious. Thinking about that day, I will never forget how happy and full I was. If I think back, I can still taste the first banana that I ever had. Even though my sister and her husband didn't have much, that trip and banana made my day and I will never forget about that.

Another time that I had been in a vehicle was the bus that transported us to the airport from Mardin camp to Diyarbakir. It was different than a car though and much more packed with people. I had a cultural shock I guess when I arrived in the United States. This would explain the phase that I was going through. Listening to English for the first time sounded like Chinese. No offense to the Chinese language, but being unfamiliar with it sounds a little weird and way too fast. I asked myself, how do they talk like that? How will I ever communicate with these people? Sometimes when people said just basic words rather than a conversation with me, I just repeated the same thing back to them.

My first neighborhood and school was Horace Mann in North Fargo. Life was good in the beginning, because I had never felt so good as a kid after four years of hell in the refugee camp. The Horace Mann neighborhood was awesome. It was my first neighborhood and everything there was perfect. The kids I hung out with, the school close to my house, Mickelson and Oak Grove Park that were a couple of minutes away, a gas station that I would go to all the time and my best friends' homes were close enough that I could ride my bike or walk. My best friends at that time were Dan (Danny), Matt, and Mike.

Danny was a little chubby guy with nerdy glasses. He was really nice, and when it came to going to his house he would give us anything to eat, except for his pop tarts; Danny did not share those with us and we sometimes snuck it out of his drawers and he would chase Matt, Mike, and I. We ate lots of snacks at his house and his parents, Tom and Jodi, were super nice to me. They treated me like I was their own son. Danny had two other siblings who were older than him. Jake was friends with my brother who went to the same school, and they played soccer together. Jake was a really nice guy and he let Danny and I play his video games all the time and allowed us to hang out in his room when he was not home. Then there was Brenna. She was tall and very beautiful. Everything about her was perfect; her long blonde hair, her colored eyes, and her smile. I had a crush on her for the longest time but never told Danny as I thought he would get upset. Besides, she was way older, too, so I had no chance but to admire her. She was a very sweet girl though.

Danny had sleepovers all the time and his parents always asked if I wanted to stay over. The family was very old fashioned and religious though. They did not have a TV and went to church every Sunday; at times they felt bad leaving me behind and took me along. Danny's dad, Tom, took me fishing for the first time. It was the happiest time ever. I really felt good because with Danny's family I was like their son and I saw Tom as the father that I did not have. Tom was a good man for being like a father figure and taught Danny and I many things.

Matt was the active, cool kid on the block. Girls liked him a lot and everybody else wanted to be his friends. He resembled me kind of but was a little paler and had brown hair. Everything about him was awesome and what I liked about him was that his parents were super nice as well. When Matt and I were together we were unstoppable. We played on the same soccer team and both of us were better than all the rest of the kids on our team and opponents that we played against. When we had soccer matches we won all the time. We owned the Horace Mann neighborhood and even kids twice our size didn't dare mess with us.

I still remember what his parents, John and Julie, did for me. They paid for me to be in soccer for many years. They bought me all the soccer gear that I needed, even shoes. I went to the lakes with them many times and they always gave me a ride to soccer practice and to the games. Matt was the oldest child in his family, with two sisters. I really liked Matt but as some years went by he chose new friends and slowly we became distant.

Mike, the red-haired, freckled one, was with us sometimes as well but most of the time he was busy. We considered him our good friend and the rest of us hung out with him when he was around. He had one younger sister. His parents were nice to us when we would ride our bikes to his house. I remember his dad Roger; he was a nice guy, always appreciating our company when we were over at Mike's house. Roger goes to the same gym as me and I see him often now. The first time he saw me there he was shocked and very happy to see me. Roger, Mike, and I went out not too long ago for a drink and it really was a good time bringing old memories back.

These were my best friends and they changed my childhood forever. I appreciated everything these families were doing for me because it made me forget about my bad days living in the horrible refugee camp. The four of us were always together, being in the same soccer team, living in the same neighborhood, and going to the same elementary school. We were best friends. These kids brought me into their homes and we broke bread together. Their families were very nice and took care of me like I was their son. Especially Matt and Dan's family. Matt's family paid for almost all my activities and I am very thankful and grateful for them giving me all those things when my family could not provide that for me. Danny's family was also very nice to me and took me to places. These two families really changed my life as a new kid on the block. Matt, Dan, and Mike showed me what childhood was like after coming from somewhere that these things were not even heard of. How can I ever forget about these families? I never will.

These families, and others as well, helped me—like my first McDonald's experience. I had never had a hamburger before nor did I know what a Happy Meal was. It sure put a smile on my face. I still have many memories from that time that I will never forget. Every time I step into a McDonald's restaurant I think of that day; I was so excited. I had heard about hamburgers and fries but I had never tasted it before which is why my first McDonald's experience was awesome. I would have to say the McDonald's first time experiment was so good which had an effect on me so much that it stuck with me till this day. When I take my kids to McDonald's I get drawn back to those days and appreciate that I can take them to a restaurant and provide them with other things they ask for. When I get frustrated or angry or need to reflect, I drive by the Horace Mann neighborhood from time to time. It helps me to be calm and see how far I have come. I still have connections with Danny, Matt, and Mike, and even though we don't see each other as much as back in the elementary days, we still keep in touch from time to time.

Our first neighborhood, Horace Mann 1992.
I'm on the far right. Dan's birthday in 1995.

All this fun and happiness would not last for long though. There were many other Kurdish families who resided in Fargo, but not close to where we were living. My mom, a widow who had no skills to find a job or drive, made us end up moving closer to these families who could provide some assistance to us.

I did not understand at that time and was very angry that we were moving. Everything was going good for me. I thought that my family did not understand how I was feeling. In the long run, though, it was beneficial for my family. I did not understand at that time and was very frustrated. We moved to a new neighborhood called the Ridge, which was a distance away, 2.4 miles away by car. Despite this, I still rode my bike to the Horace Mann neighborhood as much as I could. I tried to spend as much time with my old pals as I could but the distance was just too long. Their parents brought them to my house sometimes but because of not seeing each other so much, we became kind of distant. Matt, Dan, and Mike made new friends and so did I.

The Ridge was totally different than the Horace Mann neighborhood. It was a multi-cultural neighborhood. The ethnic groups consisted of people from Cambodia, Haiti, Vietnam, Bosnia, and Kurdistan. There was also the Ridge white kids and Native Americans. With many different groups residing in one small neighborhood like that, it caused a lot of conflict between us kids. Here we had two Kurdish groups, one was with me and the other was mixed kids that had their own group. We always fought each other. My group was always bigger than their size and many of the times those who played with them ended up with my group at the end. We all became friends often, forming the same group because many of the Ridge kids there were poor and badly mannered. They would call us names and swear at us. Maybe at times it was our fault as well, but most of the time because they swore at us, we fought them. Our English wasn't great either and that is why they tried to pick on us.

One day a big group of the Ridge kids came to our area of play. There was about eight of them, all with bikes. There were about fifteen of us Kurdish kids there. Ten were in my group and the rest in the other group. We were playing soccer against each other when the Ridge kids came to the same area. At first they ignored us and pretended not to see us. During the soccer match with the other group, we Kurdish kids got into a fight in the middle of the game against each other. After wrestling each other for a while, we quit. Our groups were dismantled as some of the kids went home fearing their parents would find out about the fight, as our parents were friends. About an hour later, most of the other group went home and there was about two kids left. Mine left also, but I stayed and still had about five kids with me.

When the Ridge kids saw that our group was small, they picked on us. Mine and the other group had about three bikes total, and they all had bikes. They would come with their bikes, swear, do something stupid, and ride off again. This went on for about ten minutes. I knew that we and the Ridge kids were going to fight each other. I sent a couple of kids to get more kids to come as we were about to fight. I saw the Ridge kids attack the other Kurdish group of three total with only one bike chasing the eight Ridge kids, all of them kicking and running off with their bikes. When I saw other kids from my group coming back, I shouted, "Hejrum!" ("Attack!") We all chased the Ridge kids away. The other group was really happy and we became one after that.

There was a good Ridge family; Kathy and her husband Gene. They had three kids: two daughters and a son named Max. Max was a friend of ours, even though he was a little younger than me. He liked me out of all the other Kurdish kids and so did his mom. There were a lot of Kurdish kids in the Ridge neighborhood at that time and most of us would always go to Max's house to hang out. Kathy would give us toys, candy, and food. She let us hang out at her house and ordered us pizza almost every day. She was a very sweet woman and was happy that we protected Max and were his friends. Gene didn't really like our company which I don't blame him now, because we were at his house all the time and there were a lot of us. The only thing that was really awkward about this family was the many pets they had. Max's family had three dogs and about ten cats. It was pretty much animal hair everywhere. Despite that it was a good place to go to and Kathy was very nice taking me everywhere they went. The Ridge neighborhood was also great because of the vast amount of Kurdish community members there. When we had Kurdish holidays and celebrations it was a great time because everyone was together and it didn't feel like we were in another country. We didn't feel left out and by ourselves, because having other Kurdish community members around gave us comfort.

We spent about two and half years there, until many families moved to either Moorhead, MN which was across the river or to other states around the country. My family didn't want to move far away, so they decided to move to Moorhead. The social services there were better. In Minnesota, families that didn't have enough income were helped out more. This was another beneficial move for my family back then who was still fairly new to the country and which needed a lot of help.

Looking back I have many memories coming to America and still remember the Horace Mann and Ridge neighborhood. I drive by the places that I first arrived in the states to reflect on my past once in a while to see what has changed. Most of the things look the same, except for things like our play area that looks way smaller now than they did when I was a kid.

CHAPTER 5

Growing Up in America

I AM FORTUNATE TO have been raised here in America, despite many hardships that I went through. Life was hard in the beginning. Trying to fit in with other kids, learning about the society here and having to deal with poverty. I never had the things I wanted as a kid. I only dreamed of having what the other kids had. Whenever I asked for something as a kid, the answer was always no. Even though I did not understand at the time, I do now. I bothered my mother and gave her a hard time for not getting me the things I asked for. My mother never had the chance to get an education. Her life was more difficult, as she became an orphan when both of her parents were killed at an early age by the Iraqi regime. Being a single mother with no education or skills made it hard for her to find a job or even drive a vehicle, let alone raise a family in a completely new country.

Our family faced extreme poverty and I used to hate going to school. All the other kids had different sets of clothing on every day and I didn't. At that time Tommy Hilfiger, Abercrombie, Doc Martin's shoes, and other such brands are what the cool kids showed off. On top of that, even though the school lunch food was free, it was not like the other kids'. They got to choose what they wanted, and I didn't. When I asked the lunch ladies for goodies such as cookies, pizza, 2% milk, the answer was no. I got frustrated and sad that other kids got to choose what they wanted and I didn't. I didn't know that I had free lunch which meant only certain basic food was given. I got upset, sad, and didn't know that my family was poor. I also didn't know that we had to pay for lunch food until later in my school years. I had school lunch during elementary school and middle school because we weren't allowed outside. However, when I got into high school I did not eat the lunch food and skipped it. Luckily in high school I was working and went out to McDonald's and other fast food restaurants that had value-priced meals which I could afford. Some days I did not have money and just drove around and smoked cigarettes. The days that I did have money I went with friends to eat for lunchtime during school.

My family moved to Moorhead, Minnesota in 1995 because of the lack of social services in North Dakota. We moved to a bad neighborhood called Romkey Park. At that time, gang activity was high in that area. There was Latin Kings, Tres 13, Vice Lords, and others. I was exposed to bad stuff being around those people. They swore, dressed improperly, did drugs, drank, and got in fights. They did other criminal activities that I was exposed to. This was definitely not a good scene to be learning from when you're only a child. Even though I tried to stay away, it was kind of hard. I was in the same neighborhood and some of those kids came to school with me. If I didn't hang out with some of them, they would pick on me and maybe even try to beat me up. So I hung out with a few and used them as a protection unit. They were constantly peer pressuring me to join their gang(s), and my answer was always no.

One day a guy named Kachoni, who was three to four years older than me, convinced the other gang members that the only way I could be around the neighborhood was if I accepted to be in their gang(s). For them the solution was to jump me. Once they did that I was automatically initiated into their gang(s). I said no and walked off. As I turned my back and started walking home, a group attacked me, throwing punches at me which made me fall on the ground and then the kicking followed. I tried to fight back but wasn't lucky because every time I got up and swung punches and kicks, they would drop me right back on the ground. It was probably a good idea to stay on the ground because there were too many of them. The jumping took a couple of minutes but it seemed longer.

Luckily I was saved by two things. One, I had a bigger brother, Khelat, and he had lots of friends with him all the time. I told him what had happened and we went to the park. He confronted those guys and told them to stay away from me. I pointed to the guy named Kachoni and told him he was the one who started everything. My brother Khelat grabbed him and said, "You fight my brother one-on-one."

Then he turned to me and said, "The only way those guys will leave you alone is if you fight the one who started it all."

Kochini was not a tall guy. He was about my height, even though he was older. Without answering my brother, I swung at that him and we rolled around in the grass. I grabbed Kochini's hair as it was long and kept on smacking him in the face. I later grabbed a rock and threw it at him, but luckily for him it missed. Otherwise I would have ended it quickly. Both me and Kochini were on the ground kicking and punching each other when I heard sirens coming towards the park. I punched him one last time and he fell to the ground. As I got on top of him he said, "Enough, cops are coming."

It was over and my brother said, "Let's get out of here quickly."

The police later caught up to us and questioned about what had happened. I told them the story, and though they tried to look for Kochini, he was nowhere to be found. Since I was a teenager, they didn't return for further questioning. The second good thing that saved me was because there were various gang members who jumped me. I wasn't really initiated into any of the gangs. It was not a single gang but multiple, and

I later found out that they jumped me for fun and entertainment only. That day was a great lesson for me, though, to not accept bullying.

Several months later we moved to a nicer neighborhood after four years of the crazy environment we were in. The newer neighborhood was farther south than where all the drama was at Romkey park. This new neighborhood was quiet, since it was next to a cemetery. At night, looking at the graves was kind of scary. That was probably the scariest thing to see from our balcony which faced right to the graves. My friend Brent was living in a house next to the apartment building there. He was a very popular kid and being closer to him was a good thing for me. I would walk to his house as it was literally a few feet away.

Later, in the year of 1996 during Independence Day, a riot broke out at Romkey Park. There was a huge confrontation between the police and the people residing there. Fights broke out and the riot turned ugly. The people at Romkey Park vandalized many police cars and were later arrested. I think this was the end of the Romkey Park violence. Starting my freshmen year in 1999, I did not hear about Romkey Park anymore which was talked about often and many people even were scared driving, walking, and riding their bike by it. I believe the City of Moorhead had contacted the landlords and questioned who they were allowing to come to the neighborhood. I also believe the strict policy of the city led to those families causing trouble to be evicted and not to be given apartments. Even though that specific part of the neighborhood was still hostile for violence and police calls it became better throughout the years as the bad people left the neighborhood.

Despite the violence being gone and the Romkey Park neighborhood being better than it had been, it still had an effect on my personality. Spending time with those kids that had a bad influence on me and being in an unhealthy environment gave me a bad attitude. Slowly I came back into the normal society, finally pulling up my baggy pants and not acting so gangster even though I wasn't one. The effect of Romkey Park made me think later in life that I had to act aggressive, that this was the way to protect myself from other kids so they would fear me, instead of pick on me. Eventually though, like I said, I grew out of it.

Growing up in America wasn't all that fun. I mean I had my good days but being poor and exposed to gang activity at an early age was not good for me. Good thing I always had a strong support network. My family constantly lectured me. For kids to like me in school I acted funny at times and protected other innocent kids which helped with my reputation. In middle and high school I became a very popular kid. My problem was that I did not know how to keep my fame. I would constantly try to defend my friends who didn't deserve to be defended. This resulted in picking fights with older kids that sometimes the battles were tough to win.

I had good friends in high school, even though I hung out with the potheads more often. After my pothead buddies made me mad over some incident, I hung out with the jocks for a while. They liked me a lot and I liked them. I went to their parties which were awesome. They were super rich and their parents loved me. I had a car and most of them could not drive. Even though I had my permit I drove them around most of the time. That didn't last too long, and my pothead friends would encourage me to hang out with them again.

Going back to their circle was probably the worst choice that I made. Most of them I helped that got their reputations to be cool kids. Later in high school, these pothead buddies would backstab me once again and that would be the last of them.

After high school was over I asked myself over and over why I had hung out with those potheads. They got me nowhere and every time my reputation was skyrocketing they always seemed to bring it down. I guess it was all a lesson for me to learn. There is a Kurdish saying that you won't become the best unless you make mistakes. Later, a lot of innocent kids that I had gone to high school with were doing drugs and smoking pot in college. At this stage I was already past this phase and it didn't cause me to make those wrong choices later in life.

Many of the innocent friends choose to smoke pot and party hard in college. If you look at it in my personal view is it should be the other way around. I may be wrong but I think it's better to make mistakes when you are young rather than when you are old. In college, people are supposed to be smart, right? Ha, I guess that is a conversation for another day.

Sometimes I ask myself how life would be if I grew up in this country in a different way? If I had the money, clothes, good neighborhood, educated parents, and had played sports. What would be different? Would I be a better person? Where would I be in life compared to where I am now? How would things look and turn out differently? These are questions that run in my mind all the time. One thing for sure is, even though I saw poverty, crime, and not enough opportunities as a kid growing up in America, I am still very thankful for what I had. I am thankful for still being a part of this country.

I believe most things happen for a reason. From my point of view, in order to see the good, one has to see the bad first. Having seen the bad at an early age, I am a better person today. Learning from my mistakes and appreciating everything that I had is what kept making me a stronger and better person. On top of it all, growing up in America would have been tougher if I didn't have the right support network. I thank all those who helped me and didn't give up on me, especially my family. I think I am a better person because of my experiences. Learning from those experiences and reflecting on them to see how I could bring change is what made me better.

I also asked myself how I could better myself by not repeating the same mistakes. These are some of the things that have made me stronger. I saw successful people all the time and I could not figure them out. How were they so successful? Having studied a lot of successful people I became aware of how I could work on my own life. Growing up in this country gave me the experiences that I needed to be a better person for the future. Having grown up in this country, I have seen what people have done for themselves to be successful. Making the right choices, work hard, and stay active leads a person to happiness and everything they want. Good comes to those who do good.

Romkey Park days.

CHAPTER 6

School Years

ELEMENTARY SCHOOL WAS my favorite. I did not know the English language but I really tried hard in learning. Also, that time was more fun—lots of activities, field trips, and recess time. During this time friends at this age were not that judgmental nor interested in 'status'. If I had a good conversation with a student one day I would probably end up at their house after school, either playing video games or riding our bikes around. During elementary school I found myself as a leader. I lived in the Madison neighborhood, or what is known as the Ridge now in North Fargo. Back then we had lots of ethnic groups living with the already established Ridge people. Some of those Ridge people were very welcoming and nice. There was a few that were very unwelcoming and brought us lots of trouble.

I was leading my friends everywhere as a child in elementary. We were always a big group of twenty-plus kids all playing at once and at times fighting one another or others kids. Though at all times, all the kids looked up to me. I was the last decision maker, and this would have a great effect on me in the future. I was born to lead but at that age I had not realized my talents and the role I was supposed to take. Everyone wanted me to go to their house and at this age it was good to lead and have so many kids look up to you.

From the Ridge neighborhood my family once again decided to move. This time things would change and I would be exposed to a new environment. We moved to Moorhead, MN in 1995. I started fifth grade in the middle of the semester. The kids at first were skeptical of me and were distant for the first couple of weeks. After about a month, things looked better and I was starting to make friends again. The following year when I went back to school for sixth grade, things looked different. I saw some kids dress real baggy and start to skateboard which they were getting lots of attention. I started to hang out with those kinds of guys and changed my style to be like theirs. I was then known as one of the skaters on my skateboard roaming the streets of Moorhead and Fargo.

Little by little I started to get attention and lots of it. By the end of the year I was one of the most popular kids at Robert Asp Elementary school. It was a good feeling to have lots of friends. By the end of the school year in sixth grade I went to a party that a girl named Amanda had at her house. Amanda at that time was very pretty and had lots of friends. Only cool kids were invited to her party and I was one of them. The party was really fun and I got my first kiss, from Amanda.

At that party there were two other girls from my school. One was named Alissa and the other was named Ashley. Alissa was half-white and half-black. She was very beautiful and liked me a lot. Ashley was also pretty—a blonde and blue-eyed girl but more popular than Alissa. They both liked me and wanted to be my girlfriend. I chose Ashley over Alissa, which was a mistake. Ashley was a rowdy girl and just hanging out with her one night she ruined my reputation. Ashley wanted attention and said a lie about me. All of the girls got mad at me for I don't know what. Anyways, to keep things short, my reputation was damaged because of Ashley. I got really mad and stopped talking to her. I tried to get Alissa's attention afterwards but it was already too late. Alissa also ignored me because she was mad that I chose Ashley over her; I don't blame her.

If I had made Alissa my girlfriend and stayed away from Ashley, my reputation would have not been damaged.

When I got to middle school, things were changing. My friends in elementary school started forming groups—popular, unpopular kind of thing. I had to really protect myself at this time as bullying was everywhere and there were older kids in the same school that one had to be aware of. Since I was in seventh grade and shared the same middle school with eighth graders, this made it a little tough. My tactic was to be silly and a goofball. I was disruptive to the teachers many times and to other students to get others' attention. Even though I did not mean it. I had to do this for the other kids to look up to me in thinking I was funny.

At times I wanted the kids to fear me rather than pick on me. I got into fights with older and bigger kids while protecting my friends, which got me suspended and sent to the principal's office many times. Having my friends' backs by fighting their fights and being a goofball helped with my reputation. I was enlisted as one of the continued popular students. Though this got me into a lot of trouble with the teachers and led me to getting poor grades in my classes. Most of the teachers were super awesome and laughed and joked with me. However, there was a few teachers that didn't think I was funny and gave me bad grades and didn't help me with my school work.

At this age I was going through puberty and started to have feelings of affection. Yet I still was new to this stage in my life and was discovering what the hell was going on with my body. I was seeing pubic hairs, getting a deeper voice, and having wet dreams. Girls looked more attractive than before and for the first time it was kind of scary when I talked to them. However, I did not show my affection to any female and acted tough.

At this stage of my life even though I was still young, providing for my family was a must. My mom could not work so we kids had to earn our own money to help with the expenses around the house. I worked at Smokey's restaurant in West Fargo bussing tables. This was my first job and the cool thing was I got paid in cash. It was a hard job because the restaurant was busy all the time, especially on the weekends. It was a job though, and I had money which made me really happy. Most of that money went to helping my mom out with the bills around the house and I did not see much of it. I told my friends that I was working and they did not believe me. A lot of the times I would be angry because there would be birthday parties and other events and because I was working I could not go. I would get off work late on the weekends and to be home around 10:30 p.m. most of my friends were sleeping. Thinking some of the parties would still be happening, I showed up but not too many people were there. It was pretty much just the kids going to spend the night at each other's houses.

Middle school was nearing an end. I had made a lot of enemies with the eighth graders; most of them hated my guts because I acted tougher than them. By the end of seventh grade most of the eight graders would come to love me. I had made peace with a few and started to hang out with some of them. Eighth grade was an awesome year for me. I was well-known by most of the kids, and I used my reputation, fear, and popularity which all worked. By the end of the eighth grade year I was starting to get nervous going to high school. There were so many questions running through my head. What is it going to be like? It is a big school, how would I be able to fit in? I had also known that there was even going to be even older kids. It was going to consist of seniors, juniors, sophomores, and I would be a freshman.

Going through high school was a challenge for me. Being a freshman, I was going to school with older kids. I chose the wrong friends in high school to hang out with. I was pretty popular and charming but I didn't use it then. I made many mistakes by hanging out with the wrong crowd: stoners and potheads. They smoked pot or marijuana all the time and heck, I was even high in class a lot of the times. This held me back from really excelling in school. I was a smart guy and caught things quickly. I loved to learn but because of my bad habits I did not care for my education at that time.

What was I afraid of? Was it being poor? Yes. Was it that I was different than the other kids? Yes. Was there too much in my head from the past trauma? Yes. Maybe these were reasons that I chose that crowd. I wanted to hide from reality because my head was racing with many thoughts. The only way that I could slow down my thoughts was to get high. This was my excuse.

Again I picked fights with older kids. My best friend Matt at that time complained to me once that he was being picked on. Some of the older kids were calling him fat and swearing at him. I felt sorry for Matt and wanted to help. I confronted the guys who picked on him. We got into a huge fight. They had lots of friends that backed them up. When I looked for Matt or my other European White Friends they were nowhere to be found. I had no choice but to use my Kurdish friends to back me up. Oh boy, did they back me up or what. The Kurdish kids that I knew were pretty badass. They chased those kids like there was no tomorrow. I lost the battle but won the war against those older kids. However, this resulted in my reputation shrinking. I used my Kurdish friends and there was not one single European white friend that helped me fight those older kids. This was looked at as an ethnic-based fight. The school got involved and many of us were suspended. The cool thing about this fight was those older guys never looked at me again. After a couple of weeks I saw Matt talking to those guys who picked on him and later he became friends with them.

The funny thing is, Matt stopped hanging out with me. That was a huge lesson I learned from. I never backed anyone up afterwards, and even though I still saw my friends get picked on, I just stayed quiet and pretended I didn't see or hear anything.

Later in my freshman year, the family decided once again to move. More opportunities were supposedly in South Dakota. We lived in South Dakota for about three years. I had to start all over again—new friends, new high school, and a new city. This was a struggle for me because I was the new kid on the block but not like the good old days of elementary but high school. Friends were already created, groups were formed and outsiders were not welcomed. I did not feel comfortable with the new kids. Losers were trying to pick on me because I was new. They didn't know me yet and who I was. For the losers it was an opportunity for them to gain a reputation and so they acted stupid around me. These were all old tricks and I didn't let anyone boss me around. No sir, I intimidated everyone who even dared to try to pick on me. They had an advantage though, because I was new and people already knew who they were.

I hated going to school. I didn't feel good or comfortable. I couldn't concentrate on my work and didn't really care about my grades. Once again I chose the wrong group to hang out with. They were cool as hell but again they smoked a lot of pot and skipped class a lot. This didn't help me with my attendance or grades. I didn't really do my work and didn't show up much for my classes in South Dakota. Heck, I even skipped lunch just not to sit with the kids in my grade. I didn't really have money for lunch either which is another reason I probably skipped.

We moved again from the first neighborhood I lived in South Dakota, resulting in me changing high schools again. During the first couple of days of my senior year at the second high school, I decided my fate. Did I want to graduate with these guys I had only known for three years? Or should I go back to Moorhead and graduate with my elementary friends? I don't think I would have graduated at all if I would have stayed. I finally decided to convince my family to move back. We did and this was the best thing that happened to me. I moved away from South Dakota, a place where I had a lot of fun but got into lots of trouble. I was doing some serious drugs and hanging out with guys who were felons. This was a good opportunity to move and start fresh again.

I went back to Moorhead in 2002 and started my senior year in September. A lot of my older friends came rushing to me, welcoming me back. I was super excited and happy to see everyone. Even though I struggled during my senior year. I had to correct and make up for all the missed work from the previous years to be able to graduate. I was going to school from 7:30 a.m. to around 6:30 p.m. most of the week.

There was a barrier coming back though because of the September 11, 2001, terrorist attacks. The tragic event made my religion supposedly a threat. I was born a Muslim and did not understand what was happening at that time. In South Dakota what was funny is that there was an African American from the second high school I went to that decided to pick on me for looking Middle Eastern. He would call me Bin Laden in class and whenever he would see me. I felt really sorry for him because he was looked at in a wrong way because of the color of his skin by other ignorant white kids. Me and some of my African American friends confronted him one day. He stopped calling me that name and actually tried to make friends with me. I ignored him, but at the same time I felt sorry for him because he did not know his own history of discrimination and oppression. A lot of old friends ignored me in Moorhead because of the political situation at that time and my religious background. A lot of them looked at me differently, and some stopped speaking to me. Again, I regret this time because I still hung out with the stoners instead of the jocks who really liked me and wanted my attention. I refused to hang out with the jocks even though they were my friends. Despite it all I didn't give up, and graduated in 2003 with my head up high. My family was very excited for me, as was I. This was a good decision I had made.

～

After my senior graduation my mother became very ill and this made me stick close to her side. I helped a lot around the house and looked after her health. It was great, because I started spending lots of time with her. She would tell me stories from the past and what she had gone through. Every day sitting with her I became wiser. She suggested I continue my education.

During the summer after high school was over, I was driving with a joint in my hand listening to 2Pac Shakur the rap artist and something hit me in my mind. I looked at the joint a little buzzed up and said, "What is this? What do I want for the rest of my life?"

After about five seconds, I threw the joint, half gone, out the window and I still haven't seen it yet.

CHAPTER 7

Getting My Head Straight

AFTER GRADUATING HIGH school, I took the fall semester off to clear my head. I got a part-time job and didn't really do anything. It was a good feeling just to relax and clear my head. I slept when I wanted to and woke up whenever. Not setting my alarm clock for a while was good. I would constantly receiving phone calls from my high school friends and others to go hang out. I always answered their calls but always came up with an excuse to stay home. For some reason after high school was over I had changed.

Back then I did not realize that I was changing but I really was. I guess I just didn't see the point of having too many friends. The friends that I had hung out with and really liked always made bad choices. Not to mention they never gave me anything. I didn't receive any benefits from them nor did I become wiser being with those friends. Most of them were always doing stupid things which got me involved being around them. Finally, I could make a choice because I didn't have to see these guys anymore. High school was over and looking back, all the friendships I thought I'd had weren't there. No one can have ten good friends; if a person is lucky they might end up having only one. What I mean by this is a good friend has your back. A true friend is kind, generous, supportive, and definitely is not stingy. It is okay to be nice to people but everyone is usually looking for their own interest. People might say they are your friends but when you need them, they are nowhere to be found. When someone uses you too much, it is obvious to tell. Also, bad friends get in the way of your vision of how you see the world. You might look at the world in a good way but they may suggest otherwise and cause a roadblock over your goals.

The good thing for me was those friends that stalled me were gone. For once I was able to concentrate on my life and goals. I had heard from other older kids who graduated high school before me saying that after high school, everything changes. Your life will change and most of the friends you had will be gone. I didn't believe that until I really experienced it. This saying was even truer when I got married later in life. Having kids also had a great effect on me later in life and really made me see the world differently, especially with my first child who brought tears to my eyes. After my first child was born I started to appreciate life. It was a good change though and I was becoming a new person.

In high school there was some really nice guys that I could have hung out with. I always chose to hang out with the punks. The skaters, the pot heads, the goofballs and trouble makers. These types of friends were bad because they did poorly in school even though most of them were very popular or so I thought at the time. Looking back I wonder why I chose those friends and their circle. They never did anything for me anyways. I was the one always defending them when people picked on them or said something bad about them. I was one of the first driver's and they were always with me everywhere. I picked them up when they wanted a ride or just to hang out. We would drive for hours and didn't stop until we ran out of gas. Some of them pitched in for gas once in a while but not often. Most of them I haven't seen for years and don't care to either. I became a better person staying away from the wrong circle of friends.

I started M-State in the city of Moorhead in the spring semester of 2004. At first I was really nervous about starting college. There were new faces everywhere and people from all over. This was a good college to start from. It was a two-year community college. Doing poorly in high school in the early years inhibited me from being ready for college. I was lucky though to be accepted, though it was a struggle trying to learn the courses and even trying to catch up sometimes.

At first I wasn't doing that great in my classes. I didn't give up, though. I studied extra hard night and day. I focused really hard and wasn't shy to ask for help. At first I went for Information Technology in the medical world, mostly coding work for hospitals. Through the end of my degree I decided to change my degree; medical coding didn't just fit into my style. I wanted recognition and saw myself leading and making lots of money. I changed my degree to an Associate of Science which I could transfer to a tri-college with the credits I received. I got my Associate of Science degree in the summer of 2006.

I would have finished faster, but I had a car accident while visiting family in Kurdistan. Kurdistan is a very mountainous region. While we were driving in an SUV down a mountain, our breaks went out. It was really hot out and I think that might have been one of the reasons. The breaks were also Chinese-made and I don't think the quality was all there. Our SUV flipped over, and my left arm was outside. The vehicle skidded on its left side while my left arm dragged along. The car accident broke my left arm and bruised other parts of my body. There was five of us in the vehicle and my injury was the worst. The others had minor scrapes and bruises. The injury required two surgeries, both of which I had done in Kurdistan. I spent over a month in the hospital which was a horrific scene.

The doctor who did the surgery came to me afterwards and said that my surgery was nearly perfect, though in order for me to have full use of my hand and arm he required me to do another surgery. The second surgery would not take place in the public hospital but rather in his private clinic. He was a medical doctor that was paid by the government. Usually their pay is very low and they have to do side jobs to make a decent living. He wanted to charge me $1,500 for the second surgery.

I was frustrated with the doctor and said, "Why you didn't just ask what I wanted to do in the first place?"

He replied, "I didn't know you were from the United States and thought you were a local that had no money."

I felt really bad—not for myself but the people of Kurdistan. Imagine how many people go disabled because they can't afford to do another operation. I had the second operation about a week later. It went well but just having to dress the wound after the surgery was very painful. The lack of pain medication also was frustrating. We are very fortunate to be in a developed country such as the United States, where everything is plentiful and accessible to us. In Kurdistan, supplies were rare and so was modern technology. You have to have lots of money to be able to get the best medical care. Being a part of Iraq, usually people have to travel outside of Kurdistan to get high-end medical tests and procedures.

I came back to the United States a couple weeks after my surgery. I got myself checked in with my family doctor and they said it was a very good surgery that had been done on me. The thing that they laughed at though was the screws and metal plate in my arm. They said, jokingly, "The screws and metal plate look like parts that you would put on a house."

When I came back to the United States I felt good being home. I knew that I would be taken care of and my arm would be strong like before. Right away with the great supplies here I was given a good dressing for my wound. In the U.S. I got a dressing put on my left arm that didn't bother my skin which I had been in deep pain from. In Kurdistan when the cloth and dressing were replaced on my arm it was so painful that it brought tears down my face. I could not move my hand, arm, and fingers when I came back to the United States. Luckily I had therapy on it, which helped me regain movement. The therapy took a while which is why I had to take a year off of college. It was worth it though because my arm was back to normal. The only annoying part being the metal plate was still in my arm and the scarring was very visible. I had the metal plate removed in January of 2015 but the scarring was still present.

After graduating from M-State I checked with Minnesota State University Moorhead (MSUM) to see if I could transfer my credits and study a bachelor's degree. The Business Administration advisor—I believe her name was Peggy—was awesome. She helped me a lot to get enrolled into MSUM and to set up my classes. This was a great university. I got to meet intelligent people from all over the world. The professors made me think in ways I never had before. The courses I took and the books I read were also good. I finally loved school and couldn't get enough of it, even though it was a struggle for me to do well because high school didn't prepare me enough. Due to not paying attention in high school and slacking all the time, it took twice as much time for me to understand a subject than if I would have listened to begin with.

The cold winter months in Minnesota of walking from class to class in college were nearing an end. I got my bachelor's degree in business administration in the spring of 2008. I was free, I felt like the whole world was mine. It was a great feeling having finished. I invited friends and family to celebrate with me. All of them were very proud of me and gave me nice gifts. What made things even more great was that I got my naturalization the same year. I became a United States citizen and now could do anything that I dreamt of doing.

I didn't know what I wanted to do after I got my bachelor's degree. I was engaged to Sheelan, my fiancée, for many years before getting married. The only downturn was that she was in Kurdistan. My whole family was in Moorhead except for one of my sister's, Dewlet.

Where did I want go? What do I want to do? Who do I want to become? Those were some of the questions running in my head at that time. I knew that I had to bring my fiancée to the United States and get married. That was the number one thing on my mind. Sheelan had waited many years for me and I had to bring her over. Second, I knew that I could not leave my family, especially my mother, as she was sick and in need of medical care. My other siblings were already married and had children of their own; it was hard for them to take care of my mother, so I was the one to help her. Third, I was very engaged in the community and doing public service work. I had non-profit experience; the Kurdish community was vast in the Fargo-Moorhead area. Lastly I continued to provide the needed care for my mother with the health issues she was dealing with, especially monitoring her type II diabetes. All these things made me want to stay in the Fargo-Moorhead area.

I brought Sheelan over in 2009 and got married on May 30th. I started a nonprofit organization called the Kurdish Community of America on September 9th, 2009, promoting cultural education and being a resource center for the community.

$\sim$

Taking several years off, starting a family while working at the Kurdish Community of America and providing care for my mother, I decided to continue my education. In August 2014, after attending evening classes at a satellite office in Fargo, I got my Master's in Business Administration from the University of Mary in Bismarck, North Dakota. The MBA I received was another great accomplishment. I knew that finally I had my head straight and was definitely in the right direction. Things finally looked normal and I was living the American dream.

College life was great and if I had the time and money I would pursue my doctorate. I had awesome instructors and professors in college. I met smart students from all over the world and I learned so much in the books I purchased for my classes. During college at times students would ask if I would like to attend their parties or hang out. I said sure but never showed up for them. I knew that friends would get me nowhere and so the only thing I really focused on was my education. I had already made enough mistakes in the past and was not going to repeat them again. I did not want to go backwards but rather forward. If I had listened more in high school, attended more of my classes and really tried to do my work I would have not struggled in college as I did. It was very difficult for me to catch up with some of my classes in college and at times felt very stupid.

Despite the struggle, I did not give up. This was my fault because I was not prepared for college in the beginning. If I would have paid attention in high school, things would have been different and college would have been much easier to deal with. Everything was good, though, and I was finally doing it: I had the right education, had a family, a house, and a career. I thank God, the United States, and my family for helping me to get my head straight and become a better person. If I hadn't stopped hanging out with the bad friends, I wouldn't be where I am today. If I hadn't started college and received an education, I would not be as smart as I am today. If I had not gotten married and started a family, I would still be chasing the world trying to find my place in it. Getting my head straight was a good idea. Sometimes it is hard to leave something behind or start a new endeavor. If one doesn't make some changes to become better, they will remain where they are forever. I am very happy to be where I am today all because I got my head straight.

CHAPTER 8

Success

FINALLY I HAD made it as a successful young man. I was a small child who came to this country without nothing but the clothes I was wearing, growing up in poverty and learning to be a man.

At a young age I helped to take care of the family by working. My first job was at Smokey's restaurant bussing tables for cash. I would collect all the money I received each night and give it to my mom to help out with the finances. This helped pay for things that we needed around the house. I was in fifth grade when I started working there. Some of the employees would question me. The employees would ask how old I was. Of course I lied about being older than I was. Even though they knew I was young, I always acted older. I acted older not just for them to think I was old enough to be working but for other reasons such as having a crush on many of the girls. There were some beautiful young gals working there. I had a crush on a quite a few of them. They were very beautiful and nice. They always gave me a ride home when I needed one and we sometimes had a conversation during the ride home, and I would tell them about my past.

The owner Obed, or his nickname, Smokey, was a very good man. A tall man in his early sixties, Obed was no ordinary man. He was as American as one can be. He was an old veteran that fought in the Korean War and always had some stories to share. He liked hard workers and didn't like those who slacked off. He was very tall and strong. When one would shake his hand it was like shaking a piece of steel. Obed didn't let customers get out of hand at his restaurant. When some would get rowdy in his restaurant, he was his own security. One time, this guy was bothering everyone at the restaurant because he was so drunk at the bar. Obed asked him to leave several times and the guy didn't listen. He thought he was tough and came face to face with Obed. Obed gave him one head butt and that was it. He knocked the guy out cold and carried him outside by himself. When Obed came back inside everyone clapped during that incident. That story would go around that nobody messed around in his restaurant and bar. After that, when he asked someone to leave, they left without questioning him.

Obed was our protector then and employed most of our family members. He knew we were hard workers. Whether it was washing dishes, bussing tables, cooking, hosting people, or serving, we did it all. He was very happy with us. One day, an employee tried to pick on me and pushed me. The employee was about thirty years older than me, a heavier guy and very tall. I was really young and he thought by picking on me that I would stay quiet. So the employee and I got into it one day and he tried to chase me. I had him cornered in the kitchen so I grabbed a steel garbage can, jumped, and smacked it over his head. The employee was shocked and didn't think I was able to do that to him. He walked right back in the kitchen area and started cooking again without saying another word to me.

Obed called me to his office. I went in there and thought he was going to fire me. He looked at me and said, "You made me proud today." I asked why, he replied, "Some of those guys in the kitchen keep questioning why

I hired your family and I would tell them, 'You will find out'. What you showed them today is that you're a tough bunch."

I was happy to hear that Obed had my back and he asked me if I wanted the other guy fired. I told Obed, "No, I don't want that, and I'm sorry for what happened. It won't happen again."

This was a true man; a guy who knew good from bad. A guy who knew hard workers from slackers. I worked at Smokey's for many years on and off until it was closed around the year 2003.

I have seen tough times and tried my best to assimilate into American culture and society. It can be tough when you are looked at as being different. Especially in an area where much diversity is not there, or at least back in the nineties it wasn't in the Fargo-Moorhead area. I went through tough times; backstabbing friendships, fake love, drug experiences, and not preparing for the real world by slacking off in school. I bullied other kids in my neighborhood and school because I was afraid to be bullied myself. I am sorry for what I did and apologize to all the kids back then, but it was nothing personal. The bullying was never physical, yet still laughing and making fun of some of those kids makes me regret what I said to them. If I could go back, I would apologize but if they remember me and read this book maybe they will understand my situation during those times. Even though it is not an excuse, it is simply an apology for the past.

Despite it all, I had made it. After high school was a new chapter in my life. I went from being a person with nothing to one with everything; I had several college degrees, I was running a successful community organization that has impacted the Fargo-Moorhead area and the Kurdistan region with humanitarian aid, I got married and had kids, I was making my family proud by accomplishing so much and living the American dream by owning my own house.

My family told me at an early age, stop, stop, and please stop all the bad things you are doing. I never listened then but I do understand now. It was their love and support that got me through those tough times. It was they who lectured me every day and helped me to succeed. Of course, if I hadn't pushed myself and made some hard changes things wouldn't have progressed and turned out for the best. Where I am right now would have been different if I hadn't pushed myself to make some serious changes and stop some bad habits.

It was not all just my family who made me a good man; I have to give myself credit as well. In this world we are tempted by so much. We smoke weed to get high because it is a good feeling. We drink and get drunk because it is a good feeling. We do other things that satisfy our desires because it makes us feel good. We choose the wrong friends because we enjoy their company. All these things may help an individual for the time being but will get them nowhere. To keep a job and to be safe, doing drugs will not help. To be productive in life and wake up every morning fresh and alert, being drunk will not help. To make love to different people often will not help being STD free. To stay away from trouble by making the wrong friends will not help staying out of it. If a person wants to change, they have to change their habits.

Being successful is up to each individual. With each bad choice one makes, the chances of success get slimmer. I say this because of my personal experiences. I tried to satisfy all of my desires by making the wrong choices. I did most of these things to make me feel good for the time being but it was not reality. When the high and rush is over, guilt takes over.

The love that my family gave me, not giving up on me, is why I am the best I can be today. Especially my mother who was there with wise words and support. Every time she lectured me I thought I wasn't listening or didn't care but it was sinking into my head without me noticing it. I took the information and her preaching in and understood where she was coming from even though I showed that I didn't care. I thought to myself, 'She doesn't know how it is,' because she was not with me all the time. Whether she knew how it was or not, my mother still played a great role in seeing me become successful by lecturing and preaching me to make the right choices. She sometimes knew what I was doing and tried to educate me on how I could be better.

Coming this far, it is not over for me. This is just half of my life's journey. I am a new person, I have lost so much but gained much knowledge on the way. I am only going to be better, not just today but tomorrow. I see myself as Columbus of America, trying to find the right opportunity to land. I have been successful because I always had this motto in my head. The future is ripe and waiting for me to shine. I have read, watched and listened to books, videos, and speeches on people's success. I have listened to successful people's advice. I believe in everyone's stories of how to be successful—but those are other people's lives and their stories. No one can make another person successful. It is up to each individual to write their own book or choose their path in life. It is the choices that each individual makes every day.

Everyone has two options. One option may make you feel good for the time being, but what about the next day and day after and the future? They say it takes up to a decade to build a reputation and only a second to destroy it. Why destroy a reputation that one has built so greatly? Find your own success if you haven't already. Don't give up! Life is too short to not dream big. Successful people may be the masters of telling their journey to success; however, each individual is in control of their own life and what comes in and what goes out. Only an individual can make themselves become successful.

A person has to learn from their experiences, mistakes, and successes to try to be better. Failure to take small steps to making changes to be better will make it impossible to achieve anything. If you want to better yourself by quitting a bad habit, you can try to cut down instead of quitting all at once. Taking small steps is better than just saying you will do something and not fulfilling that obligation. Most people eventually go back to their bad habits after saying they will quit something, such as smoking. Instead of saying 'I will quit and that is it', try to cut down on your cigarettes and eventually you will not crave them as much anymore. This is just one idea. One may say 'I want to get into shape.' They say, 'Okay, I will hit the gym tomorrow or next week.' Tomorrow comes and you're not at the gym. The next week comes and you're not going to the gym still. What a person can do instead is try to exercise little by little. How can one do this? Try going for small walks at first—five, ten, or twenty minutes. Eventually, the walks will be longer and longer distances and sooner or later a person will be walking for hours. The walks may lead someone to running. This will make you want to swim afterwards. Eventually you're at the gym hitting the weight machines.

My advice, even though you can have your own goals and ideas, is to look at the world in a big way. Think of it this way, how many people were born successful? Not many, right? People who are successful have worked their butts off to be where they are. I am not talking about an 8-to-5 job where you go in, work your hours, and come back home. I am talking about doing the 8-to-5 job but also thinking of other ways to progress. Coming up with a business idea, writing a book, running for office, doing a hobby, or things similar to that. The possibilities are endless. Everyone has potential to be successful. With the right choices and the right mentality, anyone is destined for success.

Even though you may have made mistakes, it is okay. We have a Kurdish saying that in order to be better you must make mistakes. Learning from those mistakes is what will make you better. Not repeating the same mistakes will make you better. Try to learn every day and have an open mind. Learn about a new culture, a new language, a new custom, and it may potentially lead you to a new career and perceiving the world in a new way. If you think you're not good at using your hands, maybe you should try it out. Save some money by doing your own work. If you have enough money, let someone else do your dirty job and focus on creating something new that will be more beneficial to you and the world.

Our lives are very short and time flies. Let's make it better for ourselves. Let's try to be successful. I am not saying that one might become the next president of the United States or Bill Gates of Microsoft. Though, what is success? Is it only that those holding these positions are successful? The answer is no. Anyone can define success in their own way. You don't have to be Bill Gates or the next president of the United States to say you are successful. Having both of these jobs and being in these positions is possible but hardly likely so look at the basics of being successful. If you have a good job, a good family, a house, an investment, wealth, a business, or anything that makes you happy then guess what? You are successful!

If you don't have these things, then plan better and don't give up. If you have your hand out, you are not successful. If you don't depend on anyone and have the basics in life, you are successful. You don't have to be a millionaire to be considered successful or have all the college degrees. Success is being in a better situation than you were; one that makes you not only happy but thankful for what you have. Most of us want a mansion to live in, a Ferrari to drive, enough money to never work. How likely is that? Not very. Try to be thankful if you have the basics because remember this, no matter how bad your situation may be, someone else is in a worse situation than you. If you remember this it will make you strong and you will be thankful and hopeful for the days to come. Try to be thankful for what you have because it will take you far and appreciate much.

At any given moment in anyone's life, things can turn around and be better. If you are poor, do something different to be rich. Choose different friends, read a business book, attend some kind of training, or learn a new skill. Look at your life and see where you are. Can you make changes? If you are not able to make many changes can you at least make some to be better from where you are? If you don't think you are smart, then instead of watching TV all day or just hanging out and wasting your time, read a book, learn a new skill, watch documentaries, use your hands, and most importantly, learn about the world. Are you not athletic or in bad shape? I know that the excuse for many people is that they 'don't have time to go to the gym.' Well instead of sitting for one hour straight, get out of your chair for five minutes and just stretch or walk around. Can't get to the gym? Go for a walk. If the weather is bad, go shopping. You don't have to buy anything just pretend you are interested and walk around the store.

There are many other things that a person can do to be successful. My success has been learning every day. No matter what it is—learning a new language, a new culture, food, business, technology, labor work, mechanics, etc. Whatever it is, I try to learn whatever I come across.

Most important to success is learning not to repeat the same mistakes. A person can be tempted very fast into doing things that will not only ruin their reputation but will hold them back from being successful.

I see myself as a successful person because I have learned. I learned to become better through my experiences and the bad habits I was doing. I realized that the bad things I was doing was not going to get me anywhere and so I quit doing them. Once I quit the bad habits, things turned out differently for me. I was becoming a better person day by day. The good experiences that I had, I tried to make them better the next time around. We only get better if we practice repetition; this makes us masters of whatever it is we are doing.

I remember when I hated school. When I was at school I did not want to learn or care about what was going on. Most of the days I went to school only because I had to. Once I really put my mind into my studies, I started to enjoy learning. Before liking school, my mind was elsewhere and that is why I didn't care about learning. Once I really focused on my studies, I wanted to continue to learn—and not just for a minute, but every hour, day, month, and year. I didn't stop educating myself until I earned my Master's Degree. I will continue my education, whether it is by getting another degree or continuing to being self-taught.

In my personal view, I became more successful because I started a family. A person has to know in life when to settle down. We only get older and not younger. Having a family makes a person focused more on life. A lot of times we are tempted to do things that are wrong or unhealthy. When we think about our families, we think differently and most of the time we put them first. This makes us rethink a situation and prevents us from making those bad choices.

Appreciating everything is why I am successful. I remember when I was a refugee living in the Mardin camp. I lived in a tent where I was cold and hungry. Today I have a roof over my head. I am warm and I have all the food that I want to eat. I remember living in a housing project. I drove around nice neighborhoods and dreamt about owning my own house in the future. I got that opportunity by owning my house. I am proud of myself because it was like an impossible dream. I remember when I was broke all the time; I never had money, and when I did, I spent it right away. Now I have plenty of money because I know how to manage it. If we spend our money like crazy and buy unnecessary things, we will never have enough money to satisfy all of the important things that we actually need. If I hadn't worked my butt off and had not changed, I would not be where I am today. I am successful because I said no more bad habits. I am successful because I asked myself how I can be better not just today but tomorrow and the next day. Success is in each person's hand. By making the right choices, anyone is destined to see success.

CHAPTER 9

Looking Back

Looking back, I have been through a lot. Despite all the hard times I went through, I have learned from the past and learned from my mistakes. I have learned how to become a better person by reflecting on my past experiences and journey. I experimented with drugs but realized it was getting me nowhere, so I quit. I knew it was not going to get me anywhere and the high only lasted for the time being. I bullied other kids who were weaker than me, but I quit. I knew that all people wanted the same treatment as I wanted. The way I was picked on at an early age made me pick on others weaker than me, and I came to know that what I was doing was wrong.

When I picked on other kids, I saw in their eyes a reflection of me when I felt sad or defenseless. I realized that it was wrong and thought about those who took advantage of me—those who judged me for being different. While I bullied I thought it was okay but realized it wasn't. I tried to be nice to those I bullied in high school but I had lost their trust. I felt bad but knew that I could not change anything. So moving forward I knew that I had to be nice to everyone.

I spent money like crazy while having good jobs and working many hours. Even though my checks were decent, I never had money because I did not know how to manage it. I would get my paycheck on Friday and it would be all gone by Sunday. My gas tank in my car was always on empty and I never had money to buy food when I was hungry. Even though I had a job and was working I was always broke and in poverty. Looking back now I know it was my fault because I spent my money on stupid things and friends who could care less that I did them a favor. I was always looking for more money. I wanted more of everything and never had enough of anything. This was ongoing until I graduated from high school. I did not know how to save money nor how to spend it. Things got better after high school; I learned how to manage my money by knowing where it was going and how much of it was going towards what. After learning about money management I had more money than I ever had in my pocket. From then I always had money to spend on what I wanted, as well as savings for more important things.

Looking back, I remembered my roots and where I had come from. The pain and suffering that it took to come to this country. The war, losing my house, my homeland, my father and everything I knew. This helped me to reflect on my past and appreciate the present. Looking back at the things I went through helped me to make the present and future better. The friends that I had, the bad choices I made were my reasons for failure. I don't blame anyone or anything but myself. No one forced me to do anything, but the bad habits and environment I was in led me to make those mistakes. Learning from those mistakes and reflecting on the past made me a better and stronger person. I started appreciating everything good I came across after that.

~

In June of 2014, a terrorist group called Islamic State of Iraq and Syria (ISIS)—or Daesh, as they are known in the Arabic language—threatened the Middle East and the world. They had an opportunity to gain a foothold on the civil war of Syria. There were many groups or political parties in Syria that did not come to any conclusions with one another especially with Assad's regime. Hundreds of thousands of people have been killed in the civil war of Syria since March 15, 2011. ISIS promised people a new beginning, a beginning under Sharia Law or Islamic standards. Yet they were far from Islamic teachings. No one knew that they would emerge to create chaos and destruction.

At first they got thousands of recruits from the outside to come into Syria to fight the Assad regime. Once they gained territory, oil fields, and trading routes, they finally showed off their black flag. ISIS had a dangerous campaign of destruction. They started executing everyone against their ideals and how they translated Islam. They went into Iraq, taking the city of Mosul. Over forty-thousand Iraqi soldiers fled Mosul, leaving it defenseless and for ISIS to take control. Not one bullet was fired at them by the Iraqi soldiers. Almost all the Iraqi soldiers came into the Kurdistan Region of Iraq and surrendered to the Kurdish army called the Peshmerga. ISIS started their campaign of killings. They murdered thousands of people in Mosul for no reason, to create fear throughout the city and other parts of Iraq. Little by little, they started to gain ground in Iraq, taking city after city and village after village.

The world was silent and the Obama administration did nothing. Their ugly black flags were everywhere and they became the Kurdistan Region of Iraq's neighbors. The Kurdistan Region of Iraq's Peshmerga had not fought a real war since fighting the Baath party or Saddam's regime. Fighting the Iraqi Regime, the Peshmerga had an advantage because of the mountainous terrain. When ISIS attacked the Kurdistan Region, it was a different fight. Unfamiliar to street fighting, the Peshmerga lost many soldiers in the beginning to ISIS. ISIS had modern weapons taken from the Iraqi army that fled Mosul. The Peshmerga had old soviet weapons mostly taken from Saddam's army.

The brave Peshmerga fought hard but it was no match for ISIS with their modern weapons and suicide tactics. They started taking Kurdish cities and villages little by little. The city of Sinjar was attacked from all sides by ISIS. The Peshmerga tried to fight back and hold ISIS off but with the lack of air power and limited weapons they retreated. ISIS came closer and closer into other parts of Kurdistan. At one point, they came as close as fifteen kilometers to the capital of Kurdistan, Erbil (or in Kurdish, Hewler).

This is when the United States got involved. The Obama administration sent air support to the Kurdistan region within minutes. This was a big blow for ISIS as they didn't think that the United States would help the Kurdistan Region. They were pushed back but the damage was done. The city of Sinjar was occupied by ISIS; they killed thousands of innocent Yazidis, a Kurdish minority religion. Thousands of Yazidi girls and women were taken as sex slaves. Refugees from Sinjar, other parts of Iraq and Syria flocked into the safe haven of the Kurdistan Region. I was angry and upset. I could not believe my eyes about what was happening and how the world stayed silent. I thought of the days when I was a refugee, when my family fled the Kurdistan Region of Iraq because of Saddam's gas attacks and the Anfal Campaign on us Kurds. I realized that being a refugee was not fun and that many things were needed. I also knew that the Kurdistan Region was only five million in population and there were over 1.5 million refugees there. On the news, the Kurdistan Region government said they had no outside support in helping all these refugees and no modern weapons to fight off ISIS. Finally something was done after several months. Countries, mostly from western states, formed a coalition to fight ISIS by air. They also gave modern weapons to the Peshmerga to fight ISIS. At first the weapons went through Baghdad the capital of Iraq and didn't reach the Kurdish Peshmerga. When the weapons got to the Peshmerga, most of the safety equipment, especially on Humvees, had been stripped off by the Iraqi soldiers. The Kurdistan Regional government again complained to the western countries about the situation and what had been done by the Iraqi soldiers. Finally, the western countries sent weapons and aid straight to Erbil. The United Nations and other countries came to support the refugees with aid and other supplies. Though the aid did come, it was not enough to help over 1.5 million refugees. I knew that in some camps there was a great need. Not enough support and aid was being sent.

Looking back, I knew that not much was done for my family in the refugee camp. I had to do something. I had a calling to help. With the organization I founded I sent a calling to the city of Fargo-Moorhead to help through the local newspaper called the Forum. By also using social media like Facebook, a group called Duluth Rania Friendship Exchange from Duluth, MN—a sister city of Rania in Kurdistan— wanted to help. I had my plan ready for action. The fundraiser was in the fall of 2014. The humanitarian aid was focused in the Kurdistan Region of Iraq with winter supplies to refugee children. Even though we knew that there was over 1.5 million refugees in Kurdistan and that we could not help everyone, it was still important to save some. Even if it was one person or family that we could help, it was better than not doing anything.

Our focus was in the state of Duhok in Kurdistan, where most of the refugees were—close to a million. Again, we knew that we could not help all of the refugees but wanted to focus on where the most need was. After going into various refugee camp sites throughout Duhok, we found two camps in need where much was not done for them. We decided to select them for our aid distribution. As we put the article in the local newspaper, around three thousand dollars came in just about a week. People would call our office and ask how they could support this humanitarian aid. The other group in the city of Duluth, Minnesota called the Duluth Rania Friendship Exchange decided to hold an event with us. They were familiar with the exchange of cultures from Kurdistan to the United States. They wanted to help as this was important for them because of their relationship with Rania. They organized an event where we had Kurdish music, a Skype call to Rania to whom Khalid, in charge of the Rania Center for the Youth, described the refugee situation. Later we ate Kurdish food and called out our guests to support us with this fundraiser. Many leaders attended and the group was very generous in helping us to collect around thirteen thousand dollars in just about four hours.

A lot of time and energy by the committee of the Duluth Rania Friend Exchange and our Kurdish group from Moorhead went into preparing for this event. Everyone helped in making the meal to feed our guests. The rest of the money was donated by me. I donated about four thousand dollars. This was something that was very important and dear to me. As I said, looking back when I was a refugee not much was done to help my family out. I remember being hungry, cold, and uncared for by the outside. I had a calling and took action in helping these refugees. I was successful in this project and raised a total of twenty thousand dollars.

Another great thing about this fundraiser was that even though we could not raise more, after the currency exchange, it was still double the money in the Iraqi Dinar. The supplies were cheaper there as well. Before leaving I had made preparations of my departure and how the fundraiser would be distributed. Myself along with other volunteers in the Kurdistan Region were able to help around one hundred forty five families. The one-hundred-forty-five families had four-hundred-fifty-nine children. We bought propane gas, winter clothing, milk and diapers for the infants and other children.

My future brought me to a stage where I didn't look back and say, 'Man, I can't believe that happened to me and my family.' Instead of whining and complaining to the world, I took action by seeing people in need and not just saying I feel sorry for them but actually doing something that would help them. I know that I did not save the world, but I know that I made somewhat of a change and those refugees will always remember our help from the United States. I brought smiles to the face of children who did not have anything. I provided them warmth through the winter of 2014-2015. The money helped them not to just stay warm but also provided them the cooking gas that they needed to prepare meals to feed their families. I helped infants with the nutrition of milk and helped them stay clean with diapers. I was prepared to do this work because of my past experiences and learning from them, not looking back but looking at the current situation of my life and the world.

This project helped me to look at the world in a different way. I finally knew that I really did create change. I was proud that I had done something good in the name of humanity. I reflected and said if I can contribute in the Kurdistan Region, I could do it anywhere in the world where there is a need. If I have the money, power, and time I will not hesitate to continue in serving people around the world. Humans are one and we must take care of each other. This proved to be true with the help of the people in Fargo-Moorhead and city of Duluth. Let not those who think they are human take our good name by doing bad things. Humans were born to be good and we should not let evil prevail.

∼

I am learning to be a good father for my children, though I never had a father of my own. I always wanted to know the feeling of what it was like to have a father, a person you look up to and follow in their footsteps. Someone who would teach me how to be a man. Someone who would teach me the principles of life, humanity, and the world. I did not have this opportunity of having a father. I don't know how to pass it to my kids. What am I supposed to teach them as a father? I have three children now: two girls, Peyvin and Lorin, and a boy name Perwer. I hope that God gives me the knowledge, patience, and income to be able to give them everything that will prepare them to be the best human beings in the world. I will try my best in educating them and showing them the good things in life that I have seen. The last thing I can do is be supportive as they will make their own destiny. I try to spend as much time with them as I can. I buy them what they want and am very patient with them. When they call me at work or when I am away from home I feel good hearing their voices. When I come home and they jump into my arms while giving them treats and gifts, I feel like a father.

I want to be the change in the world. If I had the money and power, I would try to do more than what I can do now. I would continue to serve more people. People and countries have the money, technology, and supplies to help everyone in this world. Most people and countries are too greedy to care, though. They only care about themselves and are like a vulture preying on the weak. If humans really came together, we could possibly end hunger, disease, and wars. My goal for the future is to be a successful entrepreneur and politician. I would like to own some businesses in the near future, possibly real estate and hotels which I am most interested in.

I would also like to run for office and hold a high political position. I ran for Moorhead City Council in 2013. I lost, but it was my first time. I was very inexperienced and over-confident. I believe that I can win this time if I run for office again. If I do run again though it will not be for city council but rather something bigger. I have the talent, background, and skills to continue my public service work. How and what I will run for in the future is still undecided but it will be my last legacy in life and it will be big.

I have been blessed to have been given the opportunity to be raised in this country. To be what I want to be without being from a specific religion, class, or ethnic group. At the end of the day, here we are, all Americans. We have all come from somewhere else in the world, or at least our ancestors have. Most of us are here to make a new beginning in this country—a beginning under the Constitution, where all can have a chance for "life, liberty, and the pursuit of happiness." God bless the United States of America for protecting so many that came to this country to start a new life full of opportunities. Looking back, I know that the United States has provided a safe haven not only to my family but so many others. I must now not look at my past but the present and the future. How can I continue to do good in this world where my kids will continue to pass on the same legacy to their children?

CHAPTER 10

The Future

My future is in my hands and no one else's. To be better is to keep feeding myself knowledge and stay focused. I must continue to be in the winner's circle, as they have led me in the direction of fame and fortune. I have many goals and dreams that I would like to continue to pursue. Some of those dreams and goals may be impossible for some. For some it may even be unrealistic. If I would tell a person what I wanted, some would laugh and say 'impossible'. Yet as Audrey Hepburn once said, "Nothing is impossible; the word itself says 'I'm possible!'" This is a motto I must go by. I must be focused and determined to pursue my dreams. What is the purpose of living and not having what you want? Are only some chosen to be great? Are only some chosen to be in power and have everything? Who is in charge of our decision-making? Why should we let someone else decide our destiny? Is the world made in a way where success is only for a few, for the supposed chosen ones?

Whatever the world may be like or may seem to some, it is up to each individual to find their purpose, their passion, and not give in to anyone or anything. I know that I will not give up. I will not let friends, family, or anyone else come in my way of achieving my goals and pursuing my dreams only because they may think it is impossible or unrealistic. I want to keep moving forward in trying to be successful. I want to be a good person in this world while at the same time continuing to do my public service work. I don't want to leave this world as a regular person. I want to be what I am destined to be, and that is a great leader in serving people and the world.

When I die, which we all will, I want to leave a legacy behind. There are many great people in the past whose names and stories still remain. Their history is written and taught everywhere today. That is how I want to see my legacy, dream, and goal in the end. In the present I want to continue to pursue and work on what I am destined to be. Despite the naysayers, I am still passionate about my dreams and goals for the future.

I am stuck between two worlds, though—two places I hold true and dearly to my heart. First is the United States of America, for this is where I have lived for almost my whole life. I have friends here, a history here and most important of all is that my book and journey started here. I don't know how to thank this country. I am fortunate and blessed to have been given a safe haven and a chance to grow up here. The United States is a place where I can be who I want to be. A place where dreams become reality.

My other part is in Kurdistan. Every time I read the news and hear the situation over there I feel goosebumps running throughout my body along with pain, sadness, and anger. My father was a very patriotic man and loved Kurdistan dearly. For some reason I have something inside me that says, 'You must be the change you want to see in Kurdistan.' I believe that if I am chosen as any kind of leader for Kurdistan that I can help it become not only independent but a country that truly believes in democracy, freedom, and justice for all.

The world is a crazy place—not because the world has made itself that way, but rather because of the people in it. People are born to be good, yet many choose evil. There is so much envy out there. So much jealousy and hatred. In many countries, a family wants to be in power forever. A person with a high position wants to remain there despite others who are better than them. Look at George Washington, for example; our first president here in the United States. He started the revolution with the British and won. The people chose him as their leader and he became president. After two terms, our first president stepped down. The people insisted that he continue to lead the country. What would be his purpose if he did? He would be no different than the British monarchy.

He chose to step down because he saw the United States future as being ripe. The United States would be a new world—a place where people have the voice to choose different leaders. A place where all can have their say with their voices and votes. The people were given a chance to give fresh perspectives so everyone could be a part of the society they envisioned for themselves and children. The United States has allowed all people to be something great if they choose that legacy for themselves.

So how does my future look? I am definitely optimistic as things are changing all the time but that does not mean I don't have hope. I hope for the best and to continue learning and trying to be better. I can only train myself for what is to come. I am ready to be a leader, whether here in the United States or in Kurdistan. I will become the person who is the voice of the people. I want my kids to grow up with their father by their side. I want to be there for my current and future children every second, minute, day, month, and year for whatever it may be that they are going through. Whether it is a celebration, graduation, birthday, marriage, or whatever it may be, I want to be there for my children. I want to give my kids everything they want. I don't want to spoil them but rather make them happy and help them appreciate everything that they have.

I look into the eyes of my three kids now and find peace. This makes me wonder how I can try to be better every day, how I can be healthier, smarter, and wealthier to provide these things for them. I want to be here in the future for my children to protect them and help them prosper. If my father was around I think things would have been different. Things would have been better for me. I would see more success than I am seeing now. I am still happy though and thankful for everything especially my mother as she was like a father figure. My mother did her duty and raised us right by sticking by her children's side. My mother protected us and gave my siblings and I the future that we have today. Despite my mother not having everything, she still raised us the best way she could.

Will I remain here in the United States or go back to Kurdistan? The question is where is the best opportunity for me? If I had to choose I would remain here in the United States. I can help Kurdistan better if I remain here in the United States. I have experience here and was raised here. I know the system as well as the people. If I could do anything for Kurdistan it would be from the outside. I applied for a job opening at the Kurdistan Regional Government (KRG) in Washington, D.C. in the fall of 2015. That didn't work out and I didn't get the job. Whatever the reason was, it was not meant for me I suppose. It is sad to see the KRG in Washington not having enough staff and the right people working there. By not having the right staff, the KRG loses many opportunities from the United States. There must be the right representatives in the KRG to better persuade the public officials in Washington to support the Kurds and the Kurdistan Region. At this moment I don't see this and I hope things change in the near future. The head of the KRG in Washington right now was raised in the United Kingdom. Being raised in the United Kingdom and not the United States makes the situation difficult; a person from the UK does not know the American system or way of life, nor do they understand the people and how they think. Before this, the prior head of the KRG was another who was raised in the United Kingdom.

I think both of these individuals can be good representatives for the KRG in the United Kingdom but not the United States. We need a Kurdish American; a patriotic Kurd that knows about their history, their people, their sufferings, and most importantly, has seen these events with their own eyes being raised here in the United States. By having these attributes, this Kurdish American could do more for Kurdistan from the

United States. Not to have a big ego but I think I would be the best fit person for this position. If not me, I can guarantee that there is another qualified Kurdish American fit for this position in the KRG Washington, D.C. office.

If I don't find myself working with the Kurdish government, that definitely means I am chosen for American politics. I have great visions of seeing myself as a successful person in this country. When it comes to politics here in the United States, I love it. The people are the rightful owners of their voice in electing whomever they see fit for office. What I have to do now is only persuade them that I am a qualified candidate. I think I will run for mayor in the city of Moorhead at first. The elections for a new mayor will be in November of 2018. This will be a great opportunity for me to run again. When I ran for City Council in 2013 I was very inexperienced. I thought that I had my name out there already and people knew who I was. I was wrong.

It takes a lot of effort to win and yet, to be honest, luck helps a lot of the time. However next time I must be more prepared. When I ran for city council I did not have the right campaign funds. I did not advertise the way I should have. Most importantly is even though I went door knocking it was not enough to cover the whole ward or area I was going to represent. I thought because of public service work and being a part of a lot of boards and committees that would only do. Another disadvantage I had was that four other candidates ran for the same ward which made it a total of five of us. This made the competition intense. This time around it will be different. I will be more prepared than the last time. I will try my best to win. I will get the right support from the local businesses and the people of Moorhead. I will advertise to the fullest extent. I will be out there working hard in persuading people to vote for me. If things look bright and if I have the right income I will run for an even higher office: United States Senator from Minnesota. Hopefully this book will give me the opportunity to run for this position. If I gain the right income, I will use most of my own money to run the campaign.

I am very excited and looking forward to 2018. It will be my biggest political career. If I win, I will be the first Kurdish American to hold such an office. I will do my best to do my public service work for the people who elect me. One disadvantage that I might see is being from a different ethnic background. I am Kurdish and I was born a Muslim. The people in the city of Moorhead are for the majority Norwegian or from other Scandinavian countries. Around the state of Minnesota, it is similar in that the majority are European white Americans. Their religion is Christianity, and being Kurdish and of a Muslim background, it is going to take a lot of effort to persuade them that I am the right person for the job. I hope to God that this does not cause any wrong thoughts or opinions. I hope that people vote for the right candidate to be in office and not against them because they are different.

The Constitution of the United States strictly states in Amendment One that any person can practice any religion or no religion. Furthermore, the constitutions states, "We the People", meaning all citizens of the United States and not only a certain class or religion. Who knew that Barack Obama would become the first African American president of the United States? It was only a dream of Martin Luther King, Jr.'s to see a black president. The dream became reality. Barack Obama didn't see himself as African American but rather as a human being. He worked hard and earned his stripes to gain people's respect. Not only African Americans voted for him, but U.S. citizens of various colors, ethnic groups, and races. The people wanted change and President Obama brought it to them. This was history to be written in the books. The first African American to become the President of the United States.

President Obama will go down in history as one of the greatest presidents that the United States of America ever had. Regardless of his poor foreign policy, he was still good enough because of the economic situation that the United States was in when he was elected. It would cost the United States only more money to continue wars and start new ones. Though I don't agree with President Obama on many things I think he is still truly a good president and will go down in history as being one. This paved the way for the first women president to run for the highest office in the United States. Hopefully in the future, we will look at candidates not by their color, religion, class, or sex but rather the content of their character. We should look at what these candidates bring to the table and how they will fight for us. This is how we should vote.

The future of the United States is bright and we continue to be the greatest country in the world, but the United States is only great because of the great minds in it. Imagine if it was only Scandinavian Americans, Native Americans, whites, or blacks only? The United States would not be as unique as it is now. We have faiths from all over the world. We have races and ethnic groups from all over the world. Many people come to this country to start a new life. To start a new beginning. Those who are a part of this society and contribute in a good way should be given the outmost respect. We must not let prejudice and injustice prevail. We are all Americans here and together we are united. As Abraham Lincoln said, "A house divided will not stand."

I want to have a good future and one that is full of opportunities. I want to be able to live the way I want to live. I want to spend my time and money the way I want to spend it. I want to help people when I want to. I want to bring change and be given the chance to do so. I want to provide my family with everything. I want to see my kids grow up happy and having everything available for them. I want to continue to make my family proud. I want to keep my father's legacy alive by being someone great. I want to give Kurdistan my full support in being independent and living in peace with its neighbors. I want to be a good citizen of this country by continuing my public service work through politics and charity. These are the things I want to see in my future. With God's help, and by maintaining my focus, I can achieve anything I want. I must remain healthy and make the right choices to live to see these things. That is my future.

EPILOGUE

L EAVING MY HOMELAND and everything I knew in starting a life in a whole new world was not easy, but it was a journey to remember. A journey that I am able to share with you, the world, and my children. Coming to the United States and seeing new faces, a new culture, a new language and way of life was not only a cultural shock but a very hard situation to be in.

I managed to hang on and tried to learn, day by day. I became who I am today because I tried and learned from my mistakes. Every day was a new day to learn something. I pushed myself hard despite some setbacks. If I hadn't sacrificed many things to become my ultimate best, I would not be as great a leader in my community as I am today. I didn't care what others thought of me or if they saw my doings as failures. I turned negative feedback into positive so I could become the very best at everything I did. I became a caring person for my mother and family, and a loving father for my children and wife. What kept me focused was not friends, as they come and go, but family. Despite the many arguments between my family and I, I always looked at everything that was important and good in the family to stay strong.

Everyone has problems and as one Kurdish saying goes, 'Everyone has a toilet in their house.' In other words, there is at least one person that is dirty in the family. My wife and I had many arguments since our marriage. At times I just wanted to give up. The reason is she and I are so different. We grew up in two different societies and the way we think is not the same. Despite the many days and sometimes years I wanted to let go, I thought about my children and how they would end up if they were raised without a father. I thought the best way was just to hang on. I might see gray hairs very fast and maybe even go bald, but I must hang on for the sake of my children. Children need their parents' support and love. They need them to be there for the many challenges that they will face in their lifetime. Despite the constant arguments with my wife, my family, especially my mother, was very supportive in trying to help me deal with the situation. They tried talking to both of us and helped us find a resolution that met both of our needs. My family was there for me at all times and I have them to thank forever. They gave me the right support and nurtured me along the journey that I have taken.

I have had many close calls with death. I have been in several car accidents that were pretty bad. Another moment was recently when I had a blood clot in my left lung.

I had taken a business trip to the city of Minneapolis for work. I drove there and back, three-and-half-hours each way. During my drive back home, I received a phone call about my uncle Bedel who resided in Arlington, Texas. My family said that I needed to go home as soon as possible because Bedel had suffered a heart attack. I hadn't seen him for many years though his kids would come and visit. I drove home and right away packed again for the trip to Texas. It was going to be a long drive; there were too many of us, which made it difficult to travel. It was a long trip that lasted almost eighteen hours. Before we arrived we got the call that he didn't make it. We were sad but could not do much but attend the funeral. We arrived after the long trip, during which we had barely rested—that would later have an effect on me. At the funeral we did not go out but helped welcome guests who came to pay their respects. After about a week we came back again, driving eighteen hours. We barely rested because we wanted to come back home as soon as possible. When we arrived at home I had another event in the city of Duluth for a fundraiser. I drove there a couple of days later which was about five hours' drive each way.

There was also an incident in front my house after I came back from Duluth. Two guys in their mid-twenties were parked in front of my house. I asked them what they were doing and if I could do anything for them. They looked at me in a cocky way and talked to me disrespectfully. I became very angry but kept my cool. When I asked the two to leave, they didn't bother to listen which is when I got really frustrated. I smacked the hood of their car and said, "Get the hell out of here." They hit the gas pedal hard and drove off while swearing. I thought the incident was over and didn't think they would return. Later, a little buzzed after having a few drinks and very calm, I saw those two rushing to my house, each of them holding a two-by-four. They were running towards me and I didn't think they would do anything. They came closer and closer and I just ignored them. Then they came up to my car and smacked it. They hit the car, a nice BMW, twice with the two-by-fours. Then the two guys came at me. I didn't think these two were going to fight, but they swung the two-by-fours at me. I raised my left hand to block the two-by-fours. One of the two-by-fours managed to smack me in the left hand. I ran into my vehicle and grabbed a police flashlight and fought back with my right hand. However, fighting two people who had bigger weapons than me was very hard especially being able to use only one hand. Another setback was that I was buzzed from drinking a few beers and was not that alert. They had the advantage and had more hits on me using their two-by-fours. They thought the fight was over and were still swearing when they left.

I called some of my guys and told them what happened. They rushed to my aid and arrived within minutes. I told my guys what had happened and they were shocked and in disbelief that this happened in front of my house. My family is well-known and respected around the Kurdish community. Also, being a Kurdish leader, it was a disgrace for the two guys who were also Kurdish to pull such a move. My guys and I went to pay them a visit about twenty minutes later since they lived close by. They were outside and when they saw us, they were in disbelief. They did not believe that I would show up at their house; they thought I would just let it go. I would have let it go, to be honest with you. The reason I was so upset is that they fought me on my property. If they had the guts, then they should have fought me when I confronted them. They should have done something while their vehicle was in front of my house. They knew that I wouldn't expect them to fight me and they saw this opportunity. I learned a huge lesson from this day. I hadn't fought anyone since high school and that was thirteen years prior. I know their father very well. I remember when they still had boogers in their noses. Thinking now they had the guts in picking a fight with me. There were six of us guys but only three of us confronted them and went to fight them. We beat them up pretty bad and I was happy to get my revenge. Like I said if they had not fought me on my property, I would have forgiven them, even if they would have swung at me on the street or swore at me only.

After beating them up, I went up to their dad as he could not believe what just happened. I apologized to him and said, "We are even." I showed the two never to go to anyone's house and hit them with two-by-fours. I taught them a hard lesson that they will never forget. I didn't call the police but they did. Thinking they would put me into jail, the police asked me if I wanted to press charges on them after I told them the story. I told the police no, I had my revenge and did not want to press any charges. I took things into my own hands and handled it an eye for an eye.

Later that night I could not sleep because of my bruised ribs being hit by the two-by-fours. So I decided to go to the emergency room to get an X-ray to see if anything was fractured. Later, the doctor told me to take a CT Scan. The doctor came and asked me if I had done some traveling.

I said yes, and he said that I had a blood clot because of it. I was very frustrated and didn't understand, especially when the doctor said I had to stay overnight. At first I didn't think anything of it; I had some pain in my ribs and thought they would just do an X-ray and give me some pain medication. I didn't think of anything like that would happen to me.

The one night turned into four days at the hospital, with IV, blood thinners, and pain medication. A lot of the nurses were shocked that I was on this floor as it had mainly older patients with blood clots. This really hit home for me. When I was alone in my room at the hospital, friends and family not present, I thought, 'Man, this is it. I am not going to have the opportunity to pursue everything that I dreamed about. I am not going to be able to do what I said I was going to do. I am not going to raise my children and they too will grow up without a father.'

I was both sad and frightened. Everything was rushing to my head at once. Then I thought about a story of a woman who was a flight attendant. After being on a plane for so long she too had a blood clot that changed her life, inspiring her to seek a new career and the path of a healthy lifestyle. After remembering this story I became normal again and knew it was going to be okay. After four days in the hospital, the doctor came and said that I could leave. However I was to go to a Coumadin clinic once a week to check my blood and medication dosage. I was on it for about three months. After leaving the hospital and coming home, I stopped some old habits. I didn't smoke for about a month, nor did I drink. The recovery period made me miss a lot of good times with friends and family. I was also on a strict diet. I could not eat what I wanted to, especially vitamin K.

This was a learning point for me, though: to try to be better, to be more patient, to make better choices and definitely continue to be active and healthy. I managed to be strong, and with God's help, I got out of it. I did not give up because I knew that my purpose was not over yet. God has been great throughout my years and I know that he has protected me all along and continues to do so. I believe the incident with those guys was for my best in knowing about the blood clot. If I had not gone to the ER that night for my bruised ribs, I would not have found out about my blood clot. This could have possibly been a worse situation for me and possibly deadly. I know that I will not live forever but will not leave this world without a legacy, with God's support and guidance.

I am trying to continue to make the right choices in life. If I had done many things differently at an early age, things would have been a little different and probably better. I don't regret most things that I did because I think learning from a lot of those mistakes made me a better person. I was never to the point where I was a criminal or did anything to be called a felon. Everything I did only hurt myself and prevented me from being more successful. Though I learned throughout my journey and I am still learning today, I am only a human being and know that I will continue to make mistakes. However, as long as the mistakes do not hurt another person, I am good. Life is too short to be deaf and dumb.

For those of us who have been blessed with everything that God has given us, we should be thankful. Do not get ahead of yourself by having a big ego because that will only kill you. Be confident but always hungry to learn more about others, about yourself, and about the world. Knowledge is happiness because it may bring a better tomorrow for yourself, children, and future generations. I have seen so much pain and trauma but that is not an excuse for me to hate others and the world. I have gained that knowledge through the experiences which I learned from. I am safe today with my family and I have almost everything that I want and need. I have much thanks for this country, the United States of America. There is no way to pay it back. The American people are another group that I have to dearly thank as they gave me a roof above my head and food on the table. The American people did not make me a prince or king, yet they gave me the chance to earn my stripes and stars, which I have done.

Yesterday is gone, the future is not here yet, so think about today. Today, how can you be better? What have you seen and what would you like to see? Plan today to make that into a reality tomorrow or the next day. I can only ask you, where are you in your life today? Do you need change? Well, change. Do you need to move up in your career? Well, move up and if you're stuck, find a new direction to take. Find your purpose in life and go for it because you never know if tomorrow will come.

ABOUT THE AUTHOR

Running from chemical attacks and the Anfal campaign, or Kurdish genocide, conducted by the Bath Regime of Iraq in 1988, Newzad and his family were placed into a refugee camp in Mardin, Turkey. After harsh conditions for four years, they were finally granted refugee status by the United States government and sent to Fargo, ND, in 1992, sponsored by two Lutheran families. Growing up in the United States, Newzad faced poverty, drugs and gangs. He choose the wrong crowd and was going nowhere with his life. During his senior year in high school, Newzad began getting his life together. The summer following his high school graduation, he continued his studies, and became active in the community through volunteering.

After gaining the right education and non-profit work experience, Newzad established a non-profit called the "Kurdish Community of America" in 2009, a year after his undergraduate degree. The organization was a resource center as well as a place for the members of his community to develop themselves, while educating the broader community about the Kurds. The work expanded into humanitarian aid work overseas.

Newzad with his organization began helping refugee kids in Kurdistan Region of Iraq in 2014, raising funds to help purchase winter supplies. He helped Michele Naar-Obed with the Duluth Rania Friendship Exchange to raise money to build a library in Kobane, Kurdistan Region of Syria. In September, 2016, he helped Elind Hozan, a famous Kurdish singer, with his project of raising money for orphan children.

Newzad continues to learn from his past and present experiences while gaining further knowledge to better himself to make the world a better place. His work has impacted the city Fargo as well as Moorhead and other parts of the state of North Dakota, Minnesota and country as a whole.

If you have a project in mind or want to help collaborate with Newzad in continuing to serve people, you can email or follow up with him on Twitter, YouTube and Facebook. We trust you enjoyed this book and enjoy learning about Newzad's Journey to America, A Kurdish-American Story.

9 781681 023731